Where Beautiful Loves II

Poetry and Prose
by
Brandy Lane

Fort Wayne, Indiana

© 2024 Where Beautiful Loves II Poetry and Prose
Edited and Authored by Brandy Lane
Second editing by Reena Doss
All rights reserved.
Printed in the United States of America.

No part of this book may be used, stored in a system retrieval system, or transmitted, in any form or any means—by electronic, mechanical, photocopying, recording, or reproduced in any manner whatsoever—without written permission from the author, except in the case of brief quotations embodied in critical articles and reviews.

Published in the United States of America by
Where Beautiful Inks LLC
Fort Wayne, Indiana

ISBN: 978-1-7363268-6-2

Library of Congress Control Number: 2024901522

Photos on Pages 110, 111, 118, 178 & 179 by Vaughn Roste.

Photos on Pages 56, 85, 113, 116, 119, 121, 124, 126 (just the book covers), 134 (books only), 140, and 212 were taken by the author.

All other images throughout this book are available through Canva and Canva Pro, including three partial AI assisted images on pages 177, 182, and 183, under Where Beautiful Inks.

Dedication

For My Dragon,

Many names I have had for you—so many characters you have played in my mind. I cannot separate them because they have all morphed into one inexplicable, incomparable entity. You are more than my friend, you are more than family, and you are more than I ever expected in another human. You have become so much of an inspiration and a part of me that I cannot imagine my life without you in it. You gave me a reason to go on when I no longer wanted to, hope when I had none, and you told me you loved me when I needed to hear it the most.

My dearest, you will forever be a part of me. Every word on these pages was written for you—because of you. I have become a better person because of you. I love you with every molecule of my existence and will always hold you in my heart.

In song and sigh,
Brandy

A Letter for my Muse

My Darling,

I want you to know
that you have made a difference—
that you have changed the world,
or at least mine, just by being in it.

You have brought
much beauty to my life.

I know we all wish
to make a difference, somehow,
and most of the time
we are left wondering if we have
done anything to be remembered,
anything to positively impact
the lives of others.

You have.

You have inspired people to sing,
to write, and to be their true selves.
Actors have memorized your words
to act out what your brain conjured.

You have inspired me to write entire books
of poetry and letters of adoration...
and even further, to look at the world as
though it is through kaleidoscope lenses.

I know that doldrums have dragged you into the depths.
I know it is easy to want to shut the door and hide away.

The want to be *normal* is there, but it takes so much effort to close out all of the *feelings*.

Normal is vanilla, and though it is good—you must admit that all the different flavors you have experienced have been equally wonderful.

Sometimes, though, it is nice to have just the vanilla.

I want you to know you have inspired me. You have entered the minds', and souls' of others with your words, your kindness, and your heart.

Your words have been spoken and sung, shared, and read.

Don't stop. Your humble self will constantly doubt your importance—your ego will tell you it isn't enough.

You are, though.

Just enough...

Keep watering the garden.

My darling, things take time to grow. Apple trees take several years to produce fruit—
even longer before it is big and beautiful.

I'd say you're ahead of the game.

You make life beautiful.

Always,
    Brrrrrandy

Contents

Letters to My Maestro

Inspiration	3
Maestro	4
For Elena	6
Lilt	8
Symphony	10
Directing the Storms	14
Coloratura	16
In Love	20
Bliss	21
Phantom	22
Keeper	25
Past Lives	26
Ephemeral	27
Compose	28

My Twin Flame

Soul Mate	30
I Think of You	33
I Will Love You	34
Breathing	35
Whispered	36
Ice Age (A Sestina)	38
When	40
Dance	41
Whispers	42

Easy on the Eyes

Just a Bite 44

Just Walk Away 46

Gluteus Maximus 47

God's Playground 48

Breathtakingly Beautiful 49

Unannounced 50

Love's Potpourri 52

Where I Oft Find You 54

In My Dreams 56

Shaped Like You 57

Stealing Time 58

Unwrap You 60

God's Poetry 62

The Winged Beasts

Cacophony 64

The Bird 65

I Soared 66

Dragonflies 68

Butterfly Kisses 69

Butterflies 70

Free 72

Flaws 73

Gossamer 74

Night & Day

A Little "Hi" 76

Dreams 78

Dream Catcher 79

Night & Day continued

Golden 80
Dream 82
Beyond 83
Fill My Cup 84
Good Morning 86
Out of Habit 88
You Are 89
Being There 90

An Ageless Love

Wishes 92
Soul-Speak 93
Giggles & Snorts 94
Best of Friends 96
Grassy Knoll 98
True Love's Kiss 100
Giddy 102

All Fun & Games

No Disguise 106
Kaleidoscope 108
"Ola" 109
The Game 110
Queen of Hearts 112
Spells of Love (part 1) The Incantation 114
Spells of Love (part 2) The Realization 116
Cats on Our Laps 118
I Love the Way 120
Sandwiches & Wine 122
If I Could 124

If You'll Just Smile

All I Must Do 127
Smile 128
Desire 129
Dress Up 130
Oh, Your Smile! 131
Blue Gingham 132
It Would Be Heaven 135
Effects 136

Isn't it Romantic?

Drift 138
At My Doorstep 140
Forevermore 142
I Simply Love You 144
As I Live 146
The Way You Are 148
Wealth 150
Boisterous 151
I Can't Help It 152

The Gifts You Bestow

Nainsook 154
Awash in Candlelight 156
All I Will Ever Want 158
The Gift 159
Quarantine 160
My Favorite 161
Only One 162
If... 163

The Gifts You Bestow continued

Enough 164
Lemon Polish 166
Just One More 168
Stay 169
Fallen World 170
Romantic Daydream 172
Hard Candy 174

That Charming Bard

Storyteller 176
The Other Side 177
Outside My Window 178
Tell the Story 180
On My Mind 182
Roaming 184

A Sense of Longing

Crave 186
Tell Me Not To 188
Irreplaceable 189
1000 Miles 190
The Train 191
You are Missed 192
Chivalrous 194
Your Favorite Things 196
Like No One Else 198
An Inspiration 199
Better Days Are Coming 200

A Sense of Longing continued

Think of Me 201
When I'm Gone 202
24/7 - 365 204

The Dragon Sestinas

Dragon (Sestina I) 206
Depths of Love (Sestina II) 208
Blue (Sestina III) 210
Hell Hath No Fury (Sestina IV) 212

Where Beautiful Loves II

poetry and prose

Someone pointed out to me;

"Remember why you started."

Ah, yes, perspective.

I started writing because I found the most wonderful treasure that I could not contain within my being! I was bursting with emotion, like spring blossoms after a long winter.
I embarked on this endeavor because I found someone to love. Someone that I could unconditionally and undeniably just absolutely... Love.

I found you.

"And I still write, but not as often, because there are dams in place, ones that I wish we never built, and I can feel the floodwaters rising, pushing against them, trying to make them crumble.

No dam can still the ebb and flow of the swirling depths inside of me! Oh, how I wish to be free to flood you with love! To saturate you with abundant waves and trickle down into the hidden places! I want to envelop you within my waters and carry you off to cerulean seas.

Can you not see it in my eyes? Can you not hear my longing soul? It constantly cries out for you!

Yes, I remember, I never have forgotten. Not for a single moment... that I did this all because of love. And I always will... as long as you are in my life."

—*Excerpt is "Floodwaters" from "The Briny Sea of Poetry" by Brandy Lane*

Letters to my Maestro

*the song in my heart

Inspiration

This longing!
My heart's string
is pulled so tightly...
quivering in anticipation
for the hours I must wait
to see you again!

The air is empty, changed —
as there is no chance
it has inspired
through your lungs
in song or sigh.

Maestro

The rhythms
of this tortured organ
pounding in my chest—
are out of sync tonight,
for you are not here
to keep time.

You are not here
to slow the tempo
or play the harmony
that dances all too well
with the song
of my soul.

You are not
around to calm
the clanging cymbals,
the ringing in my ears
with your sweet words
and hushed silence.

I miss the lilt
of your hands
guiding my sounds,
my breath, my emotions
as I sing with all
my heart.

I miss the oneness
I felt with you
as I allowed you
to guide me, to use me
as your instrument
to make music.

BRANDY LANE

Inspired by:

For Elena
by Arvo Pärt

Music lilts in the balmy atmosphere—
moments hanging onto lingering notes
in the way that honey oozes from a hive;
slowly,
sweetly,
beautifully transparent.

I close my eyes and am transported—
petals snow down from lofty branches,
tickling my cheeks as they fall;
softly,
abundantly,
wonderfully fragrant.

I lie down on the soft grass below.
The floral rain covers me like a soft blanket,
enrobing me;
gently,
quickly,
completely hidden.

The breeze catches each petal
whisking each one away—
along with my wishes and forgotten dreams;
wistfully
longingly
woefully gone.

Opening my eyes as the last notes meander,
realizing I must follow those lifelong dreams
into the unknown—
bravely
courageously
without fear.

Lilt

The piano notes lilt into the air,
wafting away in waves.
I imagine what it would be like
to walk upon them,
stair stepping as they come.

Jumping from each before it fades,
like bubbles popping
as they fall to the ground.
Some big and beautiful,
others small and colorful,
some attached—
like major chords,
needing each other to exist.

As the room fills with melody,
I am enveloped in delightful
orbs of sound.

WHERE BEAUTIFUL LOVES *II*

It boggles my mind
how music can tell stories—
how it can be happy or sad,
or angry, or whatever feeling
that needs to be conveyed—
by the juxtaposition of notes;
a universal language
with emotions abound.

As the winds move the bubbles—
with frivolity or pensively,
with violence or gentleness,
the notes are manipulated by the musician
in the same way—
used to cause fear,
anticipation, or to astound.

BRANDY LANE

Symphony

My mind feels as though
it's being punished,
and my thoughts can't seem
to form many words.

I came here to try and remedy that.

It seems as though my feelings
are too much for words—
and my brain is static.
There's too much, and
I cannot even hear to think!

*It is much like an orchestra —
incessantly warming up,
and the Maestro not showing!*

A barrage of thoughts
continually interrupted by life.

Oh, how I can't wait
until the orchestra can play again,
because I miss the melodies, harmonies,
and the still, quiet rests—
when there is not a single sound.

I miss being captive
to the mellifluous sounds
and that feeling of floating on air.

*There it is,
I'm word-painting,
finally.*

A Mona Lisa smile pans across my face
into a flirty smirk with downcast eyes...

I've missed this so much!

I find peace and refuge right here...
it never fails, even when you are silent,
as long as I can pour my offerings
out to you, I am satiated.

*Like the climax in a symphony,
words flood as quickly as my emotions.*

Oh dear, why is this release
so deliciously delightful to my soul?

continued...

Even as the instruments fade,
I am still enamored,
still intoxicated,
still held by the charms
of the trumpets' sexy blare.
I am mesmerized
and hypnotized by the baton's quick pace...

Slowing...
Slowing...
S...l...o...w...i...n...g...
Then silence...

...

WHERE BEAUTIFUL LOVES *II*

BRANDY LANE

Directing the Storms

Rumbling skies softly roaring
upon the first gauzy light of day—
it comforts me as a lioness would her cub.

I cozy down and snuggle in,
finally able to stretch out in my empty bed.

I daydream about you in a white tuxedo
with a gray vest and gray bow tie,
conducting the drumming of thunder
and the cymbal crashes of lightening,
before bringing in the soft chorus of raindrops.

*Poised in hushed animation —
you pause...
waiting for the perfect moment.*

You look over to the chimes,
and nod your head, circling your baton.

The instrumentalist responds in kind,
as if your movements were the winds
causing him to play.

WHERE BEAUTIFUL LOVES *II*

In a fury, your movements hasten.
The chimes are more like shattering glass,
as the drums increase their roar.
The cymbals crash over and over,
as you finally look to the chorus to release the rain.

Shhhhhhhhhhh...
Like a barrage of water on a tin roof.
Shhhhhhhhhhh...

Relentless, empowering, the cacophony
of chaotic sounds, rhythmically coming together...

Cymbals crash one last time—the drums are still roaring,
but so lowly that you can feel them in your heart
more than hear them.

The chorus quiets a few at a time, shushing softly,
as one voice after another
sings "drip" in varying, harmonic notes.

The drums cease.
All is still but for the "drip," "plunk," "drips,"
which are becoming fewer and farther between.

All is quiet once more as you hold your baton in the air
for a precariously long pause...
Your eyes closed, your face in a look of beautiful pain—
as though your lover finally gave you release.

You bring your baton down to your side...
and smile.

Coloratura

You had me at "Coloratura,"
and blue plaid shirts.
In, "princesses surveying their Kingdom,"
and untied shoelaces.

I was a goner when you'd look at the clock (behind me),
or any time you'd look right through me.

You had me at...
holding the door,
and teasing me while I tried to
not fall on the ice.

I cried sweet tears of joy
when you showed
appreciation for a well-sung verse.

You remembered that I like Gershwin and
called me sexy, and pretty, and told me that
you loved me.

All of the rolled rrrr's and calling me darling,
the held glances and warm embraces;
the tingle of your hand as you grazed mine
and the electricity when our feet would
brush under the table...

I didn't want to let go.

Where Beautiful Loves II

I still don't want to let go.

Even though you are letting go
because you are supposed to,
and I am allowing you to
because it is the right and decent thing to do.
But it isn't what I want.

I pretend that "Good mornings,"
and the occasional game night
while sitting rather close is enough—
that you are my friend, brother, and companion.
But it is all a lie,
because you are so much more than that to me.
You are my other half,
and I don't know what I'm supposed to do with that.

Somewhere along the way,
I got lonely, and I thought that you didn't exist.
I thought that I was going to be alone forever,
and that this other person
was going to get me through life
so I wouldn't be all by myself.
He seemed to fit at the time,
so I tethered with him and started a family.

continued...

Patience is a virtue that I guess I don't carry,
because although I've raised four beautiful children,
something was always missing in my life,
and when I found you, I found me.
If only I would've waited...

But seems that you are tethered too,
to a way of life that doesn't include me.

Funny, how loving me is an oddity in your life,
not because of who I am,
but because of how others perceive you to be.
Even your family and friends question it
because of choices you made earlier in life.

WHERE BEAUTIFUL LOVES II

So now we're friends...
who sometimes snuggle close
or hold on to a hug a little longer...
we see dreams in each other's eyes,
as others cloud over because of choices
we have made.

I will always remember the way you make me feel,
how handsome you are in the candlelight,
and in the falling snow on Christmas Eve.

You are magical to me.

And it all started when you mumbled
"coloratura."

BRANDY LANE

In Love

Write me into existence,
describe each and every flaw—
the ones that make you love me
as you gaze at me in awe.

Pen down my name in cursive
as you're thinking of my curves,
and how your hands would drive them
if you ever got the nerve.

Sing with me in harmony
as we mingle notes with care,
our breathing, one, together,
as our music fills the air.

Love me like I know you do,
it is all I'll ever ask...
I don't know how much longer,
I can hide behind this mask.

Don't get me wrong, our friendship
is a blessing from above,
but there's much more on my end...
I'm admitting, I'm in love.

… WHERE BEAUTIFUL LOVES II

Bliss

Farewell is not enough
but "until we meet again,"
to sing under the heavens—
the place music began.

Wherever the winds may take us
may we always reminisce
and remember the melodies
that once filled us with bliss.

Phantom

'Twas an evening when it happened,
I was nervous and afraid...
you had me singing solfege
and mistakes were made.

Yet you chided me gently
and complimented me...
the first of many in the five years time
since you befriended me.

You became my Phantom
as Christine, I sang...
my voice belted harmoniously
above the others, it rang.

I watched your mouth intently
each movement that it made
I mirrored every motion
each syllable displayed.

I was one with you in motion,
in timing and in tune,
I could find no better way to spend
my late afternoons.

WHERE BEAUTIFUL LOVES *II*

Seeing you became a craving,
I'd leave wanting more.
I had a deluge of feelings
I needed to explore.

When I started writing you,
my heart started to rip.
The blood-stained ink within my veins
surged through my fingertips.

Everything flowed endlessly
out of my heart and mind.
It'd been so long since I had a friend
so chivalrous and kind.

You released a talent,
that had been locked away,
I'd forgotten that my feelings had
so very much to say!

So it began, this friendship
this romance of the pen,
the most sweet of any other
that I had e'er been in.

continued...

You allowed me a place to grow
with sweet company and light,
and a shelter from the storms
that came often in the night.

Stronger in my mind,
I could finally take a command,
I leaned into the storms
and took all I could withstand.

Keeper

Keeper of my heart,
composer of my love songs—
I simply write the words to go
with the rhythms you direct!

An empty auditorium
echoes the drumming of my bosom,
awaiting the sweet melody
from your lips.

My skin craves the sliding bow,
as the shrill sounds of the sweet violins
send chills across my flesh
upon the gentlest touch of your fingertips.

Past Lives

I see flashes of a past that are not of this lifetime. A melody, a painting, a turn of phrase, the feel of an old wooden door, or the smell of freshly baked bread. They feel like my own, and I can see the setting around me—where I was when I supposedly encountered each one the very first time. It's uncanny.

There are so many memories that I cannot explain, yet there is one person I recognize throughout each. Sure, you are dressed in different attire in every scenario—in some, you are quite young, and in others, a bit older. In all of them you smile at me as though I am, and will always be, yours.

I'm not sure how, but I seemed to have missed the mark this time around. The guilt I feel is excruciating. This timeline I am living is all wrong. I feel like I don't belong. I spend my days pondering how to get back to you.

Did lightning strike me? Was I catapulted through space and time? All I know is that I am drawn to you, and the magnetism that I feel with your soul—is captivating.

WHERE BEAUTIFUL LOVES *II*

Ephemeral

You are the most beautiful of flowers,
the tallest of trees.
Encompassing all I've ever wanted
right within your being.

How can these emotions be captured?

Poems and songs arrange themselves
when e'er I think of you.
Where there are no prying eyes
and I find myself free
to think whatever I desire...

Thoughts fleeting, ephemeral...
like hummingbirds in early summer—
they magically linger
as if they have no wings at all!

There, just long enough to drink of nectar,
and in a blink, disappear—
much like the fairies we were taught
to only dream about.

BRANDY LANE

I want to compose
the greater picture with you.
Where every nerve of every sense
is touched through song and artistry.
Where beauty is felt and not just seen.
I want to ignite the passion,
spark love and ingenuity.
Reaching into the hearts and souls
of all who are willing to hear
and give them that passionate,
harmonious joy
that I have within my own.

My Twin Flame

*soulmates until the end of time

Soul Mate

I met my soul mate.
He's witty and charming
loving and sweet.
He's genius-level at times
when he's not being his goofy self.
One minute, he's god-like, powerful...
the next, a playful kitten.
Mixed with utter brilliance,
is an air of cynicism.
He loves me deep down in his soul.
I know he does,
though he claims it's unrequited.

I recognized him the moment I met him.
I dreamt of him immediately that night.
I dreamt we were toasting marshmallows
around a campfire,
so innocent and sweet.

You must understand,
I wasn't looking.

I ran into him
like he was a cement barricade,
and I was going light speed.

*You see, our souls have loved
each other for centuries...*

But, this lifetime isn't fair.
This time around,
I found him too late...
or too early...
I'm not entirely sure which
because that "what if" lingers.

All I know is that
circumstances are such, that loving
can hurt sometimes—
and timing does not allow
for us to be our true selves.

There is no doubt in my mind
that he is the one that my soul longs for.

But I cannot have him.
The cost is too high
for both of us.

continued...

*Most people will
never understand
this kind of feeling,
this depth of love.*

It's on another plane altogether.

This love is not ephemeral;
it is the kind that never dies.
It may be laid to dormancy,
but it will always be there.

Maybe in the next lifetime,
we will find each other again
at the right time.

For now,
I am trying to smother the fire
that burns within...

*But now and then,
a smoke ring escapes.*

I Think of You

I don't need to know the weather outside
because inside, I'm stormy.
The swirling turbulence sends a chill down my spine.

My mind is in a fog, my head in the clouds.
I search for warmth and comfort.

I think of you.

I wrap myself in the memory of your smile
and imagine your arms wrapped around me.
The fog lifts, the clouds dissipate, and the turbulence ceases.

I am left in the quiet stillness with your soul, holding mine.

I Will Love You

I will love you with each crease that forms
along your eye's corner,
and for every wrinkle on your brow.

I will love you in the quiet calm that I crave,
when there are no more words to be spoken.

I will love you in your pain and in fleeting
moments of joy; I will constantly search for the
flash of happiness upon your face.

I will love you in gasps of laughter, and mourning
sorrow. Through each breath I take a little of me
will escape just to be with you.

Mind you, you need to do nothing.

I will just unconditionally, unabashedly,
uncontrollably love you—
even when you feel like you are unlovable.

Thinking of you
has become like breathing...
continuous and automatic.
When I try to stop doing either,
I feel as though
I'll shrivel up and die!

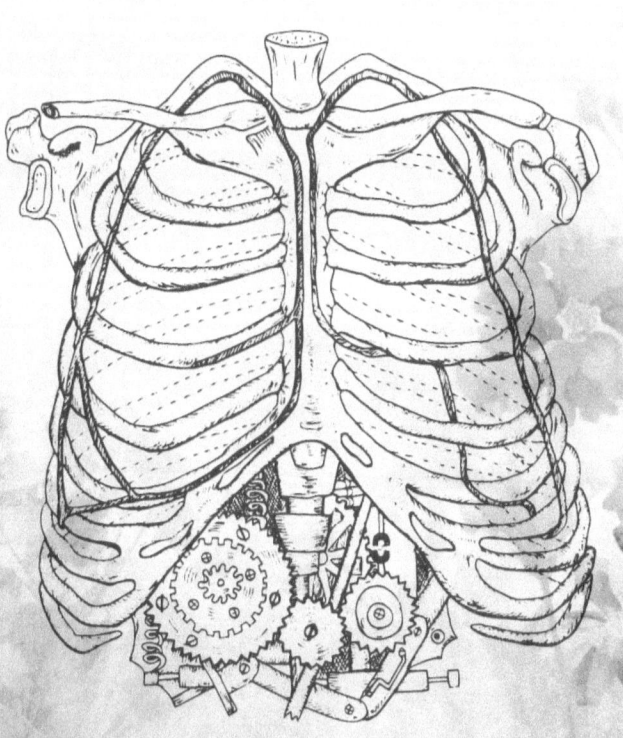

BRANDY LANE

Whispered

I left a whispered
"I love you"
upon your chest
the last we embraced.

It melted there,
between your pecs
as my lips grazed
your Abercrombie & Fitch.

Hushed not to be a secret,
but because
I nearly found myself
breathless
in your arms.

Exasperation enveloped emotions
poured out
in that pianissimo breath,
nearly lost
to the listening world...

but it wasn't anyone's ears
I was talking to;
I was saying it directly
to your heart.

Ice Age (Sestina)

Words have been frozen
locked in an ice age
impermeable,
impenetrable.
Needing the fire ignited within
to melt the rivers to flow again.

Wanting to write with ease again
and unlock what has been frozen.
Everything trapped within,
growing resistant with age.
Hearts becoming impenetrable,
thoughts, impermeable.

Though impermeable
my heart will find you again
for my soul is not impenetrable
It just stands in time, frozen
but refuses to age
still longing within.

WHERE BEAUTIFUL LOVES *II*

Oh this love, though locked within
seemingly impermeable
growing stronger with age
my heart beats again
though once frozen—
no longer impenetrable.

You broke through the impenetrable
releasing my bonds from within.
You melted the frozen,
overcame the impermeable
and taught me to love again
from age to age.

What a fantastic love to bear from age to age
with bonds that are impenetrable!
I will not not lose you again!
I just remember this feeling within
and render my heart impermeable
to doubts that make me frozen.

We will fall again and again as we age,
Our love frozen in time, impenetrable
Carried within, our bond is impermeable.

BRANDY LANE

When

When did I become afraid to tell you how I feel?
Maybe 'twas the moment that I realized it was real?

Perhaps it was the day that I discovered there was more
more inside my heart and mind than I was ready for.

Likely I had realized that you had me by the soul,
you took me by surprise and made my half a whole.

But circumstances, as they are, are somewhat in the way.
Perhaps, if we'd met another time way back in the day?

Oh, if I could have the powers to clone duplicates of us,
I'd let them take over the lives we have, that'd be glorious!

Then our souls could collide without further ado,
and we could love each other as we were destined to.

WHERE BEAUTIFUL LOVES *II*

Would it be
too much
to take a moment
to see how well
we dance together?

Whispers

I want to learn your language,
the one that whispers to me from your soul—
the one that only I can hear.

It calls to me in the night—
I hear you in my dreams,
it soothes my disquieted mind.

Easy on the Eyes

*nothing but admiration

BRANDY LANE

Just a Bite

Those earlobes!
Oh, just a little bite.
A lick, a whisper, a breath.
I want to quietly enunciate your name—
for only you to hear.

I want to purr
like a happy
over-indulgent feline.
Touching my tongue purposely
along your ear.

Those lips...
so succulent and sweet.
Just to chew on them a little
would be heaven.
Gently holding them captive in my teeth,
just enough to taste.

I breathe you in.
I'm intoxicated by your exhalations.
Your scent, like no other I've encountered.
I'm yours, just say the word.

WHERE BEAUTIFUL LOVES *II*

Those hands,
so strong and worthy.
You've worked and played hard,
you know how to use them well.
Large, yet soft and gentle,
like your demeanor.

Oh my darling!
To be held on your arms!
To trace my fingers along yours...
I am longing for you,
now.

BRANDY LANE

Just Walk Away

Most people say, "Don't walk away."
Not me, I want you to!
As many times as you'd like...
so I can stare at that view!

I'd argue if I had to,
just to get you to turn around,
or ask you pick something up
that I dropped on the ground.

I've spilled all of my secrets,
my chaste thoughts don't have a chance.
Especially, when you are wearing
that "one" pair of light khaki pants!

With that color caressing your muscles,
as you go wherever you go,
my thoughts drift to the statue of David
by Michaelangelo.

WHERE BEAUTIFUL LOVES *II*

Gluteus Maximus

Oh, there's nothing quite as fair
as your sweet, round derriere.

Many a ship celebrates launches,
but I'm just thrilled to see your haunches!

Time is measured in minutes on clocks,
(which I count) in waiting to see those buttocks!

I must admit, blushing cheeks I must hide—
when e'er I see that lovely backside.

When you leave the room, I almost don't mind
because then I can gander at your behind!

Others I see are quite inferior,
when it comes to comparing your firm posterior!

I've checked out a lot, to be honest—many
but no others come close to your glorious fanny!

God's Playground

There is so much beauty
that surrounds us;
the way the trees bloom
then grow to cool green shade—
then change varying colors,
then fall.

The designs in everything;
patterns and colors in
furs, skins and feathers...
the multitude of fragrances
from flowers and fruits
and petrichor.

But you...
You are something to behold!
From the flecks in your eyes
to the dimples when you smile,
the glitter in your hair
and the way you laugh.

That is when I realized
that God painstakingly
created all things for us to enjoy,
but he must've had the most fun
creating you.

You must've been God's playground.

WHERE BEAUTIFUL LOVES *II*

Breathtakingly Beautiful

Sometimes I can't help
but stare...
I love to look at every
shade of blue in your eyes—
the glints of silver
popping up in your hair.

The adorable dimples
that appear when you smile,
the little creases under your eyes
when you work too hard and are tired.

You are a masterpiece,
a work of art.
I could marvel for hours
and never grow weary.

You are breathtakingly beautiful to me.

BRANDY LANE

Unannounced

If you showed up out of the blue,
I would have to tell you,
"Hold on! I need to write a poem!"

Because, I've learned to extract
every pent-up emotion I have for you,
and place them into words,
and then, turn them into books.

My tongue would get tied up in twisted tangles,
and I would cry like an infant,
rendered immobile and in shock—
were you to come unannounced.

It would take all of my energy
to not leap into your arms in utter abandonment
and lavish you with kisses.
I would have to go into paralysis
to keep myself at bay.

I don't love you like most people love.
I love you with every thought in my waking or sleeping.
I love you in everything I see and wish to share with you—
as if you were me.

WHERE BEAUTIFUL LOVES *II*

I want success for you, even before my own,
and happiness in abundance
even if it causes me pain.

I never knew a love like this before you...
and nothing is as beautiful
or as heartrendingly lovely.

I can never go back to the world I knew before.
Just as when Eve bit into the apple—
and everything was realized,
I have tasted the world in ways
I never knew existed.

You opened portals in my mind to places
I had never dreamed of.
You gave me hope where flocks of it
had flown south for the winter.

Things are no longer generic.
No longer red or green or blue—
but crimson stained, chartreuse or cerulean
are the colors in my palette
with which I now paint.

You've romanticized my entire world
and made music play in my head—
as though I have my own personal soundtrack
to my life.

You, my darling earthbound angel,
you did this to me,
you gave me your wings so I could also fly.

BRANDY LANE

Love's Potpourri

Articulations of emotions,
these poems are merely
the perfume of love's potpourri.
Daily additions
of sweetness and spice,
simmer on the back burner
of my mind.

Careful of evaporation,
steadily, I monitor:
too much of one thing,
and it boils over...
not enough attention,
and it's up in smoke.

Intentionally,
and with dreamy ambition,
I breathe in the subtle
fragrance of our love.
It strengthens my resolve,
lifts my spirits
and gives me reasons to go on.

Scenting pages
and sealing them in books
for others to experience,
I share my fragranced words
so they can fully know
the love I have for you.

BRANDY LANE

Where I Oft Find You

I woke this morning with anticipation—
wanting so badly for it to be true.
I'd scheduled a trip to fly on a plane,
so that I could come and see you.

But it wasn't somewhere we usually go,
it was someplace far, far away.
Someplace no one has heard about,
is where we were scheduled to stay.

There, we could do whatever we wanted,
go for a swim, a bike, or a drive.
We could sail, or shop, or go to the zoo.
Of nothing were we deprived!

There were fruits on the trees, ready to eat!
Hives pouring with honey, too.
Cafes with frothed cappuccinos—
made 'specially for me, and for you.

Charcuterie, laid out so fine—
with nuts, and cheeses, and meats.
There was caviar and vegetables—
a whole slew of tasty treats!

WHERE BEAUTIFUL LOVES *II*

The atmosphere was perfect.
The sun shined bright all day.
Until the night—when all the stars
shone in glorious display.

The beach had luminescent waves,
which crashed upon the shore—
mimicking the stars above,
our senses begged for more.

We walked back to the resort,
I kissed you on the cheek.
We said goodnight and went to our ways,
separately that week.

Yes, my darling, I've respect,
even in my dreams.
But, the dreams within those dreams?
I've no control it seems.

Because that's where I oft find you,
in the depths of my vast mind.
You are my dream, within my dreams,
and those are the best kind.

BRANDY LANE

In My Dreams

Keep finding me in my dreams...
our excursions are a delight!
I look forward to
adventuring with you
all throughout the night.

We travel to museums,
we go to different lands.
Nothing but fun,
with my special someone,
as we escape all life's demands.

We feast on pastries and wine
on the finest cuisine, we dine
I give to you
Cuy Chactado from Peru,
you tell me, "It's sublime!"

I wish my dreams would come true...
and I really was right beside you,
'cause when push comes to shove,
you're my true love!
Without you, I'm nothing but blue.

WHERE BEAUTIFUL LOVES II

Shaped Like You

Every day is a gloomy gray
when you are not around.
I feel an emptiness inside,
so deep and so profound.

It's as if I lost a half of me,
and now there is a hole,
and filling it has since become
my one and only goal.

But you see, he's like a key,
not just anyone will do.
It seems the puzzle piece I need,
is one that's shaped like you.

Stealing Time

All this time, you were worried that
you would come crashing down from the pedestal...
the one you claim I fashioned for you.

But can't you see?
You were never on one, to begin with.

From where my broken body,
barely standing,
still adores your precious heart.
I gaze across the table
upon your kind eyes and adorable smile—
like glints of the sun off peaks of waves,
the love you have for me still glints through,
though overwhelmed with life
within a sea of chaos.

I still see you.

The glimmer of your soul, exhausted,
but still shining.

WHERE BEAUTIFUL LOVES *II*

I feel the same as you,
wanting to give so much more,
but unable to conjure the strength or the time—
as the clock ticks relentlessly toward its final destination.
What if I could steal time?

What if it's held within your lips?
Those succulent sweet plums
that hold a honeyed kiss—
as my name tumbles out of them?
The playful exchange of your glances,
not as perfectly-in-sync
as they once were with mine,
but my heart still skips a beat
when my periphery doesn't fail me.

The beauty of you...
like the comfort of a favorite blanket,
a little worn, but in all the perfect places.
I want to wrap myself in you,
crawl right into that body
and snuggle your soul—
hug you from within.

I still see you.
I still feel you.
And I never want to stop.

BRANDY LANE

Unwrap You

What do I want for a gift?
People ask me all of the time.
Anything I choose,
would not be as sublime;
as seeing you again—
and holding you in my grasp.
No, nothing could compare,
no jewels or things with clasps.

You're better than anything
that I could ever want!
Just your company,
the cute ways that you taunt.
You make me feel so safe,
and loved, and seen, and smart!
You make all of the brokenness
leave my fragile heart.

WHERE BEAUTIFUL LOVES *II*

So, all I want is you,
to make more mem'ries with.
'Cause now I know that love
is more than just a myth.
It's not full of pride or greed,
it's not a thing that fades,
it doesn't hurt, or cause you harm,
and it comes back in spades.

So, no thing with pretty ribbons,
no expensive cars.
No trips, no furs, no caviar,
no naming the heaven's stars.
The only thing that'll satisfy—
all that will ever do,
is the mere hope that someday soon,
I'll get to unwrap you.

BRANDY LANE

God's Poetry

When God was done with Earth and Sky,
with things that swim and things that fly,
He looked down from his throne on high
and pondered, then let out a sigh...

His breath formed into clouds that lay
around your forehead, streaked with gray—
that turn to silver, in sun's ray—
makes you dashing, I must say.

He's added lines over the years,
some formed from smiles, some from tears—
some from sleepless nights from fears,
that rumble 'round between those ears.

Oh, I've seen the poetry of God's pen,
and how he edits again, and again,
forms changing ev'ry now and then,
for everyone, since life began.

Your stanzas, I have memorized,
they are most beautiful, I won't lie.
So, I'll embrace them by and by,
and recite them till the day I die.

The Winged Beasts

*the ways in which you make my heart take flight

Cacophony

Birds outside
produce a cacophony,
such as an orchestra
enhancing their tune.

Bits of song
that make no sense,
but sound beautiful
when put together.

It reminds me
of all of the music
I've experienced
with you.

WHERE BEAUTIFUL LOVES *II*

The Bird

I am the bird at your window,
I greet you whenever I can,
resting at your windowsill,
watching as you plan.

You spend your days just thinking,
you create and bare your soul,
as I warble from the ledge,
cheerleading is my goal.

Sometimes I'm just the background,
sometimes the melody;
because when your mind is quiet,
it'll remind you of me.

Through cold and blustery winds,
I persist with my song,
to let you know you're not alone,
I'll be here all along.

BRANDY LANE

I Soared

Found in a cage, perhaps locked in my own mind;
I had grown comfortable there,
not aware of my own fears.
You chided me gently—coaxed me out.

I would come out and sit on your shoulder
watching from your point of view.
I let you show me bits and pieces of a world
I hadn't seen, but only imagined.

Happy there, I'd come and sing—
made it my goal to keep you company; after all,
I hadn't flown yet, just perched there
with a different view.

The day came when you nudged me off
from that lofty height.
I was shocked, afraid—a little scared,
I wasn't sure of your reasoning and was falling rapidly.

But then, I spread my wings.

I flapped around and gained some height,
I flew in circles, trying to find my bearings...
and when I reached your familiar shoulder to rest,
you looked at me—and smiled.

I knew then that it was for my own good,
that you had nothing but the best intentions for me.

So, I glanced at you with all of the love inside of me,
and with a dive...

I soared.

BRANDY LANE

Dragonflies

> Thoughts flit 'round like dragonflies with nowhere to land.

WHERE BEAUTIFUL LOVES *II*

Butterfly Kisses

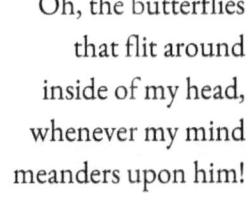
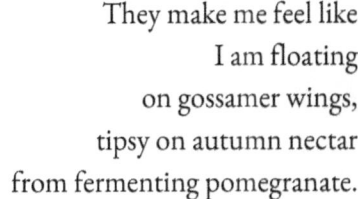

Oh, the butterflies
that flit around
inside of my head,
whenever my mind
meanders upon him!

They make me feel like
I am floating
on gossamer wings,
tipsy on autumn nectar
from fermenting pomegranate.

When he is near,
I swallow them
in one big gulp,
unintentionally—of course,
but inevitably just the same.

When we touch?
The winged beasts
flap so hard in my stomach
that they make me tremble
as the earth when it quakes.

When we kiss?

Well, I can only imagine...

Butterflies

The little blue butterflies.
I've always loved them,
dancing their ballet
around my sandals
of the same color.

The crystal-clear waters
rushing past the rocks
where they rest.
Such an otherworldly blue—
my favorite memory
of childhood summers.

*I see them when I'm with you,
in your eyes and in your soul…*

I want to chase them inside
and watch them for a while.
Your thoughts
drift around on their wings.

*I wish to examine them gently,
then let them go.*

You fascinate me,
just like those blue angels—
you comfort me with your subtle grin.

*Every magical moment
I have with you, is a salve
for my aching heart.*

I will love you like those butterflies...

letting you softly land and explore
when you so desire,
then watching you dance on the wind.

I will long for you in the winters
and pray for your return
when things are fair.

I won't hold you in glass jars—
you will forever be free.

*I only hope that when you rest,
you'll find refuge in me.*

BRANDY LANE

Free

Can I just love you from right here?
My mind is juxtaposed.
I tried to love you in real-time,
a fantasy in prose.

I want to try and capture you
like a butterfly
but things with wings must remain free
to wander—lest they die.

So I'll stay here and hold you dear,
while watching from afar...
just like the Earth still loves the moon,
more than all the stars.

I will anticipate the day
for when you will return,
much like the flowers in the spring
for which the bees doth yearn.

I love you for all of the things
I long, myself, to be;
articulate, and whimsical,
beautiful, and free.

I'll overlook all of your flaws,
each one of your mistakes,
and always be right here for you,
no matter what it takes.

I fly
effortlessly
on large gossamer wings —
as your precious words
lift me up,
I fly.

Night & Day

*I think of you

BRANDY LANE

A Little "Hi"

If only the sun
would shine again,
and chase the clouds away.
If only its warmth
would comfort me,
all throughout the day.

If only I could
sprout wings to fly,
high above the clouds—
I'd go and move
them all myself,
as much as God allows!

My wings
would glitter in the sun,
fresh with morning dew,
as I moved
those clouds around
to start each day anew.

WHERE BEAUTIFUL LOVES *II*

Alas,
I do not have wings
and so I cannot fly;
my only way
to spread some cheer,
is with this little "hi."

I pray
it makes you smile,
for it's all that I can do...
Pretend it's
wrapped in sunshine:
a gift from me to you.

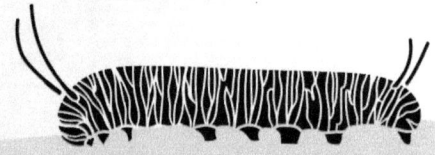

BRANDY LANE

Dreams

My imagination was kind to me last night,
in giving me time to spend with you.
In my slumber, my many dreams
were filled with frivolity and fun.

Then came the sun through my window—
were he as a soldier wrapped in glorious light,
come 'round on his noble steed
to wrestle my thoughts to the ground.

He may have taken me from my restful sleep,
but was kind enough to let me keep
the memories as though they were real,
as though I were really there.

We played games throughout the night,
and drank new wines and old, as well;
the newest being a raspberry-peach,
which was rather lovely and rather sublime.

Such a glorious time laughing we had—
and playing as we used to do.
Somehow, it's nice that the world
stripped away our burdens through solidarity.

WHERE BEAUTIFUL LOVES *II*

Dream Catcher

I dream about you often.
It's my mind's way
of spending time with you.

The other night, it was about you
being published in several magazines.
Every magazine I opened,
there it was: your name in print.

It was an odd little dream,
but it was nice seeing
how successful you had become.

Last night, I dreamt
we were walking into a movie theater,
and you held my hand.

Such a sweet, simple dream,
it made me feel a closeness
that I am missing.

I love feeling you next to me.
Even if it is—only in my dreams.

Golden

Golden glints of sun off morning dew,
eyes squint, adjusting to the light.

My heart races upon first thoughts of you,
heart flutters violently with delight.

Each day refreshes my love anew—a journey!
Butterflies take flight.

As long as you live on this earth, so blue,
I shall sleep soundly through each night.

Because you are the essence of a love so true,
there is no equal—not quite.

WHERE BEAUTIFUL LOVES II

A Beautiful Day

A beautiful day for a drive,
off wild and free.

That happy feeling of leaving the world
behind for a little while.

Windows down, with your arm out,
fingers playing with the wind—
as if it were a river stream,
cold and fast.

Music blaring, cold drink beside,
thoughts drifting
as the lines quickly disappear,
and reappear
as you speed down the highway.

Breathe in deeply, that outside air—fill
your lungs, and exhale.

This is joy, no tether, no bounds just
you and the road—until you reach
your destination.

Then the real fun begins.

Dream

If I were there beside you,
I would sing you a lullaby.

I'd caress your cheek
as you fall asleep...

and watch your chest
as you breathed in and out.

I would curl your hair
around my fingers,

and watch your eyes,
cloaked under lids

as they twitch around,
while you dream.

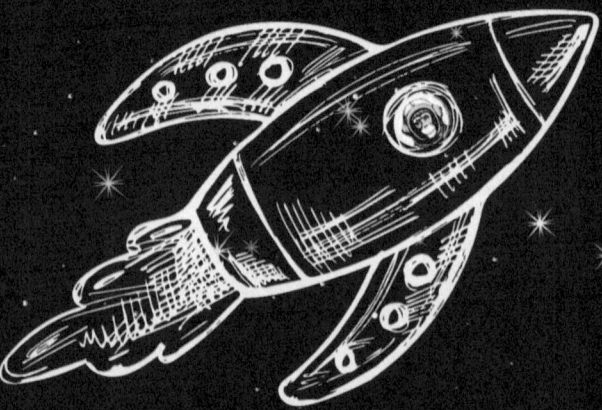

WHERE BEAUTIFUL LOVES *II*

Beyond

Sunlight kisses my cheek
like how your presence touches my soul.

Once-emptied parts of me —
now filled with light, are whole.

Breathing tempo softens,
thoughts of you calm my mind.

Imagination soars beyond
the tethers that doth bind.

BRANDY LANE

Fill My Cup

How divine
the morning time
in its glowing hues.

Today with clouds
yet I arise
to subtle grays and blues.

Dawn-light hovers,
under covers
blinking sleep away.

Suppose I'll awake,
ready to take
advantage of this day!

I'll make coffee,
perhaps tea—
either will perk me up.

I stroll downstairs,
sit in my chair,
nursing my favorite cup.

I sip and smile,
in thought for a while...
because it's what I do —
on waking up,
I fill my cup
whene'er I think of you.

Good Morning

Those little words,
to some, seem trite,
but they got me
through the night!

They tell me I've
another chance
to live and love
and sing and dance.

They symbolize
my love for you,
each day, it is
refreshed and new.

Every day,
when I awake,
I will not, you,
for granted, take.

> Good Morning, my darling!

> Coffee.

> Sounds delicious, now I need some!

When I open my eyes,
the first thing I do
is write to say,
"Good morning" to you.

BRANDY LANE

Out of Habit

It's out of habit that I wished you, "Good morning!"
—but it's a good habit I don't wish to break.

I know you're on vacation but for that one moment
between asleep and awake—when I pressed "send,"
I was only thinking about how you are still on this planet
with me and that we, even though we are not together—
are still under the same sun, moon, and stars.

We are still breathing the same life-giving air on this Earth.

And how the rain that may fall wherever you are,
will sooner or later run through my faucets —
and I will bathe in it, thankful to be alive!

Every day, I thank God for you.

So, even though I know you are taking a break from the world,
I am still grateful that you are in it.

WHERE BEAUTIFUL LOVES *II*

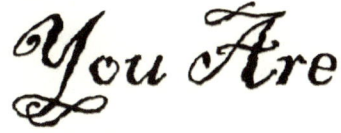

You are the coffee in my cream,
the color in my dream,
the picture in my meme.

You are the steam in my shower,
the cord supplying power,
the minute in my hour.

You are the sun to my moon,
midnight to the noon,
the one who makes me swoon.

You are the honey in my tea,
the bumble in the bee,
the cool shade from a tree.

You are the day to the night,
the landing of my flight,
my cause for much delight.

You are the melody in my song,
the right choice over wrong,
the home where I belong.

You give me hope where none is found,
keep my feet upon the ground,
makes me want to stick around.

BRANDY LANE

Being There

You are the magic
that unleashes my mind,
tethers my heart,
nourishes my soul.

You vanquish the demons
and light the fire
that shows me the way.

You are the catapult
to my many ideas
and dreams and desires,
and I am able
to try new things
with my newfound courage.

You don't even need
to hold my hand,
just you being there
is all I desire.

An Ageless Love

*if I could go back in time,
I would find you sooner

BRANDY LANE

Wishes

Oh, why can't we be
as little children and play in the sun?
I miss you...
and it's not even you keeping me away.

I feel like I'm locked in the tower!
Won't my dear, sweet dragon
come and save me?

Sigh.

I wish there were wishes to be granted,
true luck in a horse's shoe...
it would be great to find
a fairy godmother
or a leprechaun
and shake them down for their powers!

All of the many dandelions
I've blown off into the wind,
the prayers of exasperation...

I am still waiting for them to be answered.

WHERE BEAUTIFUL LOVES II

Soul - Speak

Soul-speak to me in poetry,
no reason, just pure rhyme...
All I ask is for a moment
of your precious time.

Just meet me here, and have no fear,
just see my barren soul.
The one that, intertwined with yours,
will make the two halves whole.

Know this love will always flow
from my heart to you...
and know that when I speak of love
you'll always know it's true.

BRANDY LANE

Giggles & Snorts

Only a few short hours
before I get to be
within your energy!
I'm so excited!
Okay, yes...
When I am with you,
I sometimes completely forget
that I am a grown adult
with responsibilities
and I love that.

It's the days that I feel grown
that gets me in the most trouble.

*I often wish that we
could go somewhere
and just be you and me.*

I will always treasure that ONE day
when we just talked about life,
and the future...
I loved the stripped-down to bare
emotions.

*We were all smiles
and no one else
existed that day.*

It was one of the best
hours of my life, no joke.
I wish I could have those feelings
of that one hour all of the time.

I will always remember
the way we smiled at each other.
I know the world can see
right through me now...
I cannot hide my exuberance
when you are near.

You are sheer joy.

You still freak me out though...
you know, the grown-up me.
But the kid inside?

I'm all giggles and snorts.

BRANDY LANE

Best of Friends

If I were little with no cares in the world,
I would be at your door today,
asking if you could come out to play.
We could play in the dirt and climb trees,
we could play hide-and-go-seek,
we could play make-believe,
(even better than we do now).

We would make no-bake cookies
and then catch frogs in the creek.
We could hike, and forage,
and quietly watch the forest animals.
We would get dirty and sweaty
and then wash it all off in the stream.

I feel like I knew you a long time ago...
I cannot explain it.
As if we're time travelers, we've run into each other
over and over again.
Do you understand what I mean?
Part of me is scared to lose you,
yet, another part of me
knows you'll always be there.

In person, you are still a mystery.
But not here.
Here, there is an ever-flowing connection
between my mind and yours.

I truly wish I understood what I'm feeling, and why.
But for now—
I'm just going to continue playing in the mud
and playing make-believe,
and feeling this extraordinary connection.

I'd like to think you understand.
I wish I knew that you did.

BRANDY LANE

Grassy Knoll

Would that I
could step up on your doorstep,
I would take you by the hand
and lead you to a grassy knoll.

We would...
lie upon the grass
and share the menagerie
we see in the puffy white clouds
*...roll down the hills
in dizzying laughter,*

I would place buttercups
under your chin
to watch them glow
as your eyes do
when you gaze into mine.

I can't explain
what I see or feel
every time our eyes meet.

WHERE BEAUTIFUL LOVES *II*

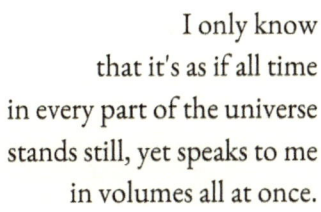

I only know
that it's as if all time
in every part of the universe
stands still, yet speaks to me
in volumes all at once.

In that moment,
nothing else matters...

it's a glorious feeling

that I beg God
to have more moments in!

*Your soul is the most
beautiful creation
I've ever encountered.*

BRANDY LANE

True Love's Kiss

I've never felt
a kiss so true,
than the one I left
upon your cheek.

You didn't kiss me back,
and it was never intended
that you would...
but in that one moment,
the unconditional love
that I have for you
was made known.

You are my dearest friend,
my companion,
my soul's missing half.

If ever in my life
I could relive
a few moments,
that would be one of them...
me,
giving you...

true love's kiss.

WHERE BEAUTIFUL LOVES II

BRANDY LANE

Giddy

What is it about you that makes me all giddy?

I know it won't be for long,
and you'll be busy,
but I get to see you today!

Gosh, this feeling?

It's like going to see
your best friend
after they've been
on vacation all summer.

It's like going
on a roller coaster!

It's like... one of the best
feelings in the world.

*When I'm around you,
all I can do is be happy.*

*You make me
the best version of myself
that I know how to be!*

I still don't know
why or how...
but I'm so totally happy
that I have the privilege
of knowing you.

You bring out every ounce of joy.
This feeling is like
being at a parade.

It's like the awe I experienced
the first time I saw the Colorado Rockies.

It's like a beautiful song.

BRANDY LANE

Oh my goodness!

You are like
a New York Cheesecake
smothered in hot fudge,
whipped cream
and a cherry.

Oooh... the mist from a waterfall
on a hot day.

A snuggly pair of thick socks
in mid-winter.

I just love being around you!

It doesn't take much
to make me happy.

Just knowing
you are in my world
makes my life
much more wonderful!

All Fun & Games

*just playing around

BRANDY LANE

No Disguise

Without you...

I'm a clock without a battery,
that cannot keep the time.

I'm a poet at a loss for that
I cannot find a rhyme.

I'm a pauper on the street corner
begging for a dime.

I'm settling for mediocre,
instead of what's sublime.

When you're around...

the time is filled with fun,
it flies!

My rhymes come more easily,
surprise!

I've won the lottery,
the prize!

I can just be me...

no disguise.

BRANDY LANE

Kaleidoscope

You are my kaleidoscope;
you have made the mundane
weirdly beautiful.

Looking through the scope,
I see a world so much more lovely
than previously imagined.

The ordinary objects
morph into geometric shapes
in every color available.

A different perspective
gifted in a myriad of designs,
when shaken… shifts.

This gift continually gives,
continually changes,
and grows more important each day.

The chaos of the objects
come to order like a mandala;
reminds me of Spirograph play.

"Ola"

… yup, that's all it takes
for my heart to do somersaults!
My hands start to tremble
and I am filled to the brim
knowing you love me.
Just knowing you are around,
makes my life complete.

BRANDY LANE

The Game

Spread out on the table,
my defenses down,
I want to be the victor,
but I need to win that crown!

Waiting for you, hungrily,
to make a thoughtless move,
so I can conquer and divide
your impressive brood.

You hesitate and grimace,
I try to shield my thoughts
by attempting to distract you
with banter and whatnot.

"What was that unexpected move?
You've claimed another land!
Ugh, you've made it twice as hard
for my realm to expand!"

"I'm totally losing this game!"
I say in exasperation,
but then remember I've got a card
to use in desperation.

"I get to remove two of your men,
and place, there, one of mine,
thank God I remembered I had this—
just in the nick of time!"

Back in the game now, much relieved,
and I'm feeling fine.
"Oh shucks," I say, holding up my glass,
"I think we need more wine!"

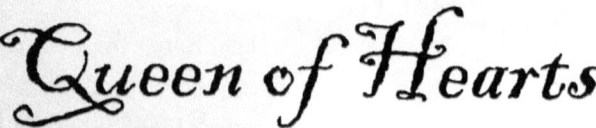

Queen of Hearts

Shuffle

Deal

Flip

Flirt...

"What was that?"

"Huh?"

Discard

Draw

Wink...

BRANDY LANE

Spells of Love (part 1)

A pinch of gristle
from a mother bear's cheek,
will give me the answers
that I seek.
Spit from a camel,
eye of newt,
please spirits, speak!
Do not be mute!

I want my love
to burn with desire,
for that, I'll need
some dragon's fire.
Some silver fur
from a winter fox,
bring me a man
with gorgeous locks!

Fresh water from
the lipid pools,
to give him eyes
like sapphire jewels.
A branch of a tree
that has been broke
to make him tall
like a mighty oak.

WHERE BEAUTIFUL LOVES *II*

A large cricket,
for musical flair.
Oh heck, make him sing—
toss a bird in there!
A dust of pollen,
rain from a cloud,
to make him fertile
and well endowed!

Honey from a hive
to make him sweet,
and for a bit of luck,
some rabbits' feet.
Wisdom comes from
an owl's downy feather;
for strength, a strip
of buffalo leather.

Now for the conjuring
of this spell;
I'll need three coins
from the wishing well!
The ingredients gathered,
I start to recite
the incantation
at the stroke of midnight.

In front of me,
he starts to appear:
the tall, dark, and handsome
man, I'll hold dear.

… BRANDY LANE

Spells of Love (part 2)

I realize I'm a wrinkled mess
in my witch's gown,
and that my old and tired face
is covered with a frown.

Too late to fix the way I look
before he comes to fruition,
my only hope is that he has
a charming disposition.

Our eyes meet, and he looks
deep within my soul.
My other half is finally here,
so I can now be whole.

As he takes me into his arms,
his fingers trace my face.
He tells me I am beautiful,
my frown is now erased.

He tells me not to worry,
that he'll care for me somehow...
with that, the furrowed wrinkles
vanish from my brow.

My looks begin to soften,
the more he speaks to me,
somehow his love sets
my inner beauty free.

WHERE BEAUTIFUL LOVES *II*

*Bewitched, bothered, and
bewildered,
I will him forever adore —
for he now has me
under his spell,
now and forevermore.*

Cats on Our Laps

I have never had
a sweeter relationship than ours.
It's one of the most precious, endearing,
priceless encounters that I've ever had.

I've never felt this much emotion
for anyone in my entire life,
it's overwhelming but completely welcomed.

I could just eat you up!
Oh. My. Gracious!

What is it that draws me to you,
makes me want to protect you, comfort you,
tell you everything will all work out in the end?
I'm always comforted in your presence,
I'm sometimes like a little girl around you,
and you're like a precious little boy.

It's so funny how I feel
all of time in its generations
when I'm with you.

I can imagine us young and playing in the puddles,
or college-aged... picnicking on a grassy hill
under a shady tree.

I can imagine us when we're too old to care
about anyone's opinions and saying whatever
we darn well please... oh wait, that's you now!

*I can see us watching sunsets
whilst sipping tea on the back porch,
with cats on our laps.*

BRANDY LANE

I Love the Way

*I love the way
you make me feel inside.*

Like, when the ice cream truck
comes down the road
in mid-summer.

Like the electric air that comes
before a big thunderstorm.

Like that moment
when you walk into a room
and everyone yells, "Surprise!"

Like when you're rolling down
a grassy hill with your best friend.

Like when you see the view
after climbing a mountain.

Like understanding what an artist felt
as he painted with his brush.

*The feeling that somehow...
you become alive, and real,
like the Velveteen Rabbit.*

Where every sense comes alive,
every pore, every nerve ending
feels something.

*A dreamy existence where
you don't want to ever leave.*

A safe, comfortable place...

I'm there right now,
lying on my bed...
writing to you.

BRANDY LANE

Sandwiches & Wine

Good morning my sweet darling,
I trust you had good sleep!
The morning sun shines strong today,
through the window, it does seep.

I dreamt of adventuring to lands
far away from here—
with you, of course, beside me,
oh, my darling, dear.

We saw wooded lands and chapels
dotting the countryside,
we picnicked along a river,
after a long carriage ride.

Feasting on wine and sandwiches,
we talked for quite a while.
Oh! How I've longed to spend some time
seeing my favorite smile.

Out in the middle of nowhere,
we passed the time away,
gazing into each other's eyes,
while on the grass we lay.

After all, I am just dreaming,
and you're not really here...
and I'm reminiscing of a moment
that never happened, I fear.

WHERE BEAUTIFUL LOVES *II*

So in anticipation,
I must wait quite some time,
and hope someday that it comes true—
that by a stream we'll dine.

I'll patiently be waiting,
praying time is on our side,
that someday I will be with you
in the countryside.

Dotted with the chapels,
cottages, and lands,
and we can someday escape
from all of life's demands.

In the meantime, I'll keep dreaming
'til the timeline aligns...
until the day I spend with you,
eating sandwiches and wine.

BRANDY LANE

If I Could

If I could, and you were free...
I'd pack a picnic for you and me.

We'd settle by a quiet lake,
I'd reach out for your hand to take.

We'd have fruit and cheese and bread and wine,
and enjoy the gorgeous day, divine!

We'd laugh and appreciate the view,
you'd gaze at me, and I at you.

We'd reminisce the days gone past,
and how they flitted by so fast.

You'd lay your head upon my lap,
so you might take a little nap...

as I brush my fingers through your hair,
tousling it with the greatest care.

I'd glide my fingers down your cheek,
to find the smile I often seek.

That handsome grin I've grown to know
that tells me that you love me so.

If You'll Just Smile

*the many ways I try

to get that beautiful simper

across your face

WHERE BEAUTIFUL LOVES *II*

All I Must Do

All I must do to smile
is think of any
of the many times
we've spent together.

There are some days,
you just being there
carries me through.

You are always someone
I look forward to seeing you;
there is never weariness
or hesitation.

There is no one
in my world,
other than you,
that can stake that claim.

BRANDY LANE

Smile

It's time for me
to walk a bit
in the valleys of my mind,
to frolic with
the hummingbirds
and meander in the columbine.

The sun is rather
bright today,
I squint my eyes to see
the bluest skies,
just like your eyes,
each time you look at me.

I cannot help
but grin inside
when e'er I think of you,
but several times a day
I wonder,
if you're smiling too.

Oh, your smile!
If I could wake up to just
simply that every day!

WHERE BEAUTIFUL LOVES *II*

Desire

My dreams get me
through the night,
but what shall get me
through my days?

I long for your touch,
the gleam in your eyes,
your cherubic smile,
and oh! those dimples!

The constant
of you on my mind,
lacks in tangibility!

I want your soul
gazing upon mine!

I long for
the chemical reaction
that happens throughout
my body when you're near!

I love the way
you make me feel!
There is nothing I desire
more in this world.

Dress Up

You are the most
beautiful creature I've ever seen,
every inch of you is perfect.

The icing on the cake, however...

is when you dress up.

I'm not talking about coiffed hair
or suit and tie, none of that matters
(although there is that one pair
of khakis that make your tush
look like the backside of
Michelangelo's David)...

No, I'm talking about your simper;
the way your smile creeps across your face
from one side to the other
until you are beaming!

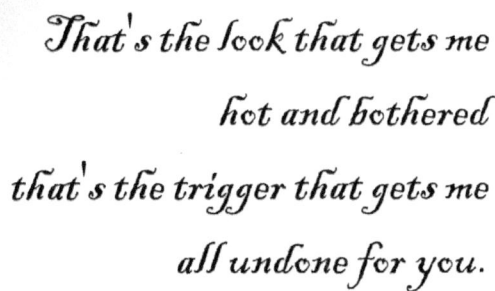

That's the look that gets me hot and bothered that's the trigger that gets me all undone for you.

My only goal in life is to make sure you look your very best every day, so I will do everything in my power to keep you grinning.

BRANDY LANE

Blue Gingham

My brain works mysteriously,
the way it ties things together
memories with patterns or rhythms,
songs, and emotions.

A scent or a tune
causes my mind
to travel back in time
in a matter of an instant.

I'm in the middle of packing
as my eyes settle
on the interior of a box
a friend had dropped by.

I keep staring
at the blue gingham
that lines it,
and feel oddly comforted.

WHERE BEAUTIFUL LOVES II

My first thought
is that it is from
Bath and Body Works...
that must be it,
as their fragrances
have been a part
of my routine throughout
my adult life.

I keep staring at the box
and catch myself in a grin.

There is only one thought
that makes me grin in
that particular way...
just like him,
one side of my mouth
ahead of the other.
A little sly, a bit coy.

Blue gingham was the shirt
that he used to always wear...
it was the one
that made me notice
his beautiful eyes.

BRANDY LANE

I'm suddenly transported
back in time,
his rolled up sleeves
and handsome face.
His silvery hair
and that gorgeously rich laughter.

I'm shuffled into a wanting mode.
I want to lavish him in love.
I want to write to this man I adore,
for no other reason than I want to.

I want to show him so much that I care
and insist on writing him books of poetry
to let him know…
to let the world know,
that he's absolutely wonderful.

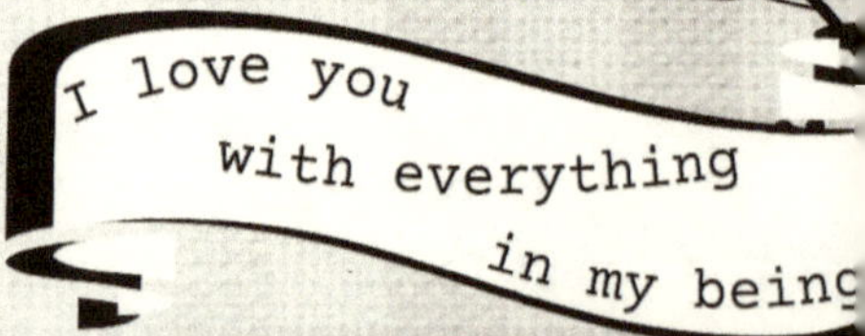

Page after page,
hour upon hour…
but I don't mind
because
I love him.
(But especially in blue gingham.)

WHERE BEAUTIFUL LOVES *II*

It would be heaven
if I could just simply hold
you for a little longer,
gaze into your beautiful eyes
and get to soak in
everything about you.

Effects

How natural it is when my thoughts of you place a most relaxed smile across my face.

How beautiful it is when my heart beats in anticipation whene'er it knows I will see you soon!

How wonderful it is when my soul bounces around inside of this body, trying to get to you.

How fortunate it is to have someone in my life that makes me want to continue on, makes me want to do better, makes me strive for greatness, to never settle.

I am not sure how or why you have these effects on me. All I know is that I'm bathed in a wash of comfort and well being when it comes to you.

Isn't it Romantic?

*I must admit —
I get a little carried away

Drift

Snuggle down
comfy,
soft,
in blankets of warmth.

Thoughts drift
happily,
contemplative,
with memories of you.

Wishing time
evasive,
 elusive,
would slow to a crawl.

Wanting to
replay,
rewind,
moments spent with you.

Sweet glances
coy,
sweet,
filled with joyous love.

Feeling warmth
hugs,
fingertips,
as you embrace me.

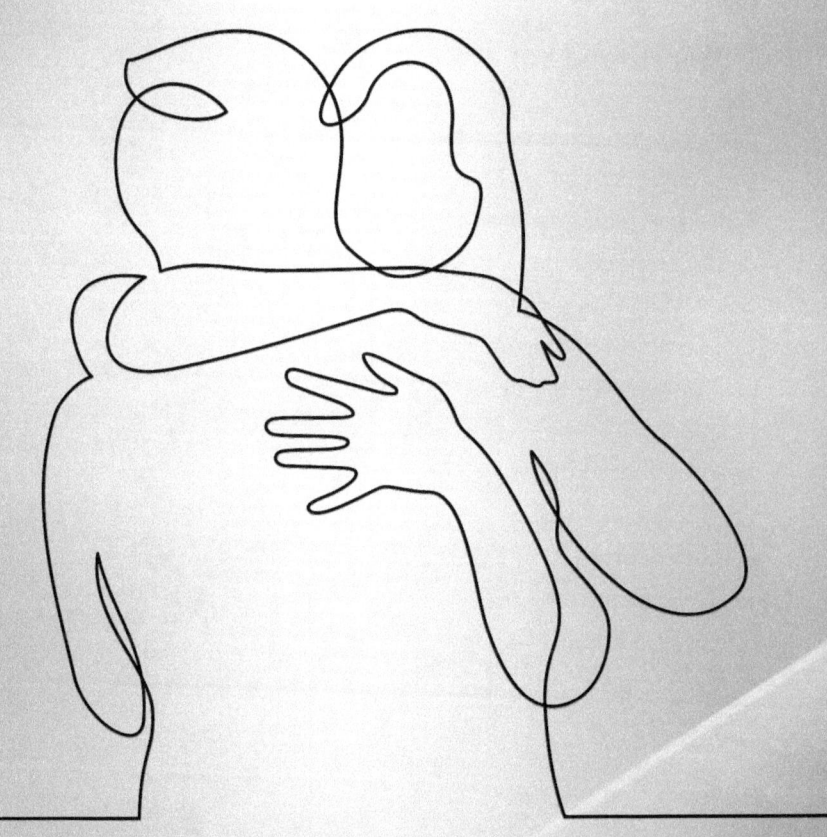

BRANDY LANE

At My Doorstep

Ruby red and bittersweet, the wine
passing over my lips,
splashing on my tongue,
flowing down my throat.
It hits my stomach,
then my veins,
I feel it coursing to my brain.

The thoughts are already there,
covered under blankets.
I shall toss them off, for they are
hot and cumbersome.
Yes, freeing thoughts I tuck away.
I look around in despair,
but find you are not there.

You, to whom I look up to—
I'm left like a chorister
without a director.
Oh just give me the time,
I beg you, I implore—
so that I know the score!

WHERE BEAUTIFUL LOVES *II*

My hand sits empty, open...
wanting yours to hold
the longing I feel,
the wanting...
my soul's companion...
I'm waiting here,
just longing to have you near.

Oh, this *want* to be near...
Only two glasses, I swear...
but this wine,
thoughts of fingers entwined...
a closeness beyond compare!
Your boyish glance
leaves me entranced.

Liquid courage,
give me mere moments
to princess up and prepare.
Brush my teeth,
moisten my lips,
coif my hair.
To meet you there,

at my doorstep.

BRANDY LANE

Forevermore

A writer, poet, lover of words
sat down upon the floor,
he grappled with his heart—
full of love, forevermore.

He pondered carefully,
before penning down his stories,
painting poems, spinning yarns,
and inking allegories.

Somewhere in his mind,
somehow, she was always there...
on ships, on trips, her name on his lips,
his darling, oh so fair.

Persevering to find new places
that she and he could travel...
e'en if only in their minds
the adventures could unravel.

If not a destination,
they could travel to a time:
either present, past, or future...
to moments most sublime.

As long as he could be with her,
through each imagined endeavor,
he knew he'd always have her love.
Unconditional, eternal, forever.

I Simply Love You

To know that for a moment, or even a brief while,
that amongst the sea of chiseled faces and beautiful derrieres,
I held your gaze long enough to know that you loved me.
Though fleeting, it pierced my heart for eternity,
and no one will ever see me as you did.

To know that even though I will never be your cup of tea,
you played the Mad Hatter for a while to appease my inner Alice.
Playing rounds of Hearts while painting our palates red with wine.
I feasted on your compliments, never making me feel smaller,
only perfectly adequate.

I knew that even though I wasn't what you expected,
what you *knew* you never wanted;
that you still cherished me and loved me to the core.
I knew because I felt the same;
perfectly imperfect, unconditional love.

That hasn't changed—for you still are my favorite dream.

Pinch me! No wait - just a few more moments before I must awake.
I don't wish to wake up from the days of chatter and song,
of red lips and pretty dresses—
of you in all colors of blue that brings the oceans in your eyes alive.
I don't want the feasts and games and silly banter to fade...
just yet.

WHERE BEAUTIFUL LOVES II

I have said it before...

*"I never knew I needed you,
and now I don't wish to be without."*

I think you must not believe me, but it's true!
You are part of me now.
A part that I would be broken without.
You are beautiful and magical,
a transformative part of my life.

And I simply, love you.

BRANDY LANE

As I Live

It's your whispered breath
across my neck that I wish to hear
carrying sweet compliments to my ear.

Oh, how I crave the way you used to stare!

Your large hands
gliding down my back as we embraced,
exploring a little further than a typical, friendly hug.

Breathe me in,
and exhale how you love my perfume!

Gaze upon me again like you would the Mona Lisa
and exclaim how pretty you find me!

Say my name again with fire in your belly
and rumbling on your lips
and remind me again and again,
how very much you love me!

WHERE BEAUTIFUL LOVES II

*Because you once showed me
where beautiful lives…
and I want to relive it
over and over again —
not just in dream or memory,
but as I live and breathe.*

BRANDY LANE

The Way You Are

You know my heart.
I love your mind and your soul.
I always hear you speaking to me
in a language no one else seems to hear.

You are with me, always.

I am the best version of myself
when I'm in your company.

You are a dream... forget the pedestal,
I've had you in the heavens this entire time!
You need no pedestal when you can fly.

As my dragon, you cannot fall!

You soar among the clouds
and rise above their shadows!

You always have me looking up,
which is the best place.
Maybe that is why I think of you
in the ways I do!

You are larger than life,
and even when I go to comfort you,
I'm still looking up at you.

Even in a heap,
even at your lowest,
I will always look up to you.

My admiration
does not include perfection.
Because your imperfections
are what I admire most.
To me, your flaws are endearing.

Don't ever think
you are less than.

I love you
just the way you are.

BRANDY LANE

Wealth

How I'd love to wander
among the fields of green...
you could be my king,
and I could be your queen!

Flowers would bow down,
as we meandered by,
drenched in beams of gold,
the sun, envious in the sky.

Your hair, a titanium crown,
mine, a coppery gold...
your eyes, a proper sapphire,
hint at stories to be told.

My lips, as red as rubies,
teeth as ivory keys,
sing songs of love for you
in simple melodies.

We'd gaze upon our wealth,
our love, the greatest treasure...
for it is in your eyes I see
a kingdom beyond measure.

WHERE BEAUTIFUL LOVES *II*

Boisterous

My brain thinks he's magical,
mystical, DaVinci-like.
He's timeless—
and his dimples and stormy clouds of hair
make him distinguished and gorgeous.

Why does my brain think he's so glorious?
He pushes me aside most of the time,
but in those moments
when he takes time to spend with me,
the universe stands still.

Everything in the world falls away, it is just me,
crowned as a princess with my boisterous dragon.

We rule kingdoms together.

I think my mind keeps him as a dragon
because I can love him with no regrets...
he's under a spell in this life, I cannot have him.

He's a beast, a metaphor.

I cannot help but smile when I think of you.

The Gifts You Bestow

*how you affect me with your presence

BRANDY LANE

Nainsook

I wish I could compose a song
with threads of the softest cotton.
Drop it light around your shoulders
to comfort and sustain.

If hope could be a gift,
you would have a pile
of packages at your doorstep,
but you'd have to open them
and not refrain.

If I could be a comfort, a hiraeth,
a place to rest when you are weary.
I should hope you'd find me
your joy be unconstrained.

Wanting to love freely,
with no strings, unconditionally...
giving everything I am,
pure love should not be contained.

Everything within me: hoping,
loving, giving, comforting.
My soul, my heart,
my body, and my brain.

*All are free for the taking,
my gifts to you, my friend...
for through sharing my all with you,
all I lack is gain.*

Awash in Candlelight

I want to write of last Christmas Eve,
but how do I properly capture the moment
burned into my memory?
Oh, to wander back in time one year!
The candles lit, the lights dimmed,
and all I could focus on was you,
up on the balcony, in the soft glow.

If I were an artist,
I would paint that one moment.
You, just sitting there—a masterpiece.
Your handsome face, your hair, you dressed all in black...
I had never seen you look more dashing.

I'm tearing up even now,
with the memory of how awestruck I was,
gazing up at you,
knowing I already had been given
one of the best gifts in the world
in knowing you.
I try not to lavish on you as much as I used to...
but those feelings never wane.
This longing is always in my heart.

I refrain from many things I want to say,
but my darling... my heart still calls your name,
my mind still adventures always with you.

WHERE BEAUTIFUL LOVES *II*

As bittersweet this decadence may be,
as I long for honeyed words
and milky glances as you used to.

Time moves painfully fast,
yet achingly slow,
for the anticipation that I have
that does not leave me.
I still can hold
the mere magic of those rare moments,
however few...
so intense and compact
that they still hold their power over me.

I don't wish this to ever end,
I don't wish to hide my feelings from you—
as it does nothing but torture my soul.

I had to write this letter,
because I had to clear my thoughts,
because every time I think of Christmas Eve...
you will pop into my mind—
all awash in candlelight.

You took my breath away,
I tend to always find myself
having to remind myself to breathe...
even now, just thinking of you.

All I Will Ever Want

Snowflakes bunched together,
cascading down in gentle thuds,
smashing on my eyelashes
and melting on my cheeks.

Christmas Eve services ended,
we walk to our cars,
marveling at the glistening crystals
glittering the streets.
It crunches under our feet.
One last hug before we go our separate ways.

I hold the large envelope in my hand.
"Do not open till Christmas morning!"
I don't need to open it at all,
although I will, come morning.

I already got what I wanted for Christmas,
and for every Christmas yet to come!
It didn't come wrapped,
or with any pomp or circumstance,
but it is and always will be my favorite.

All I will ever want
is you.

WHERE BEAUTIFUL LOVES *II*

The Gift

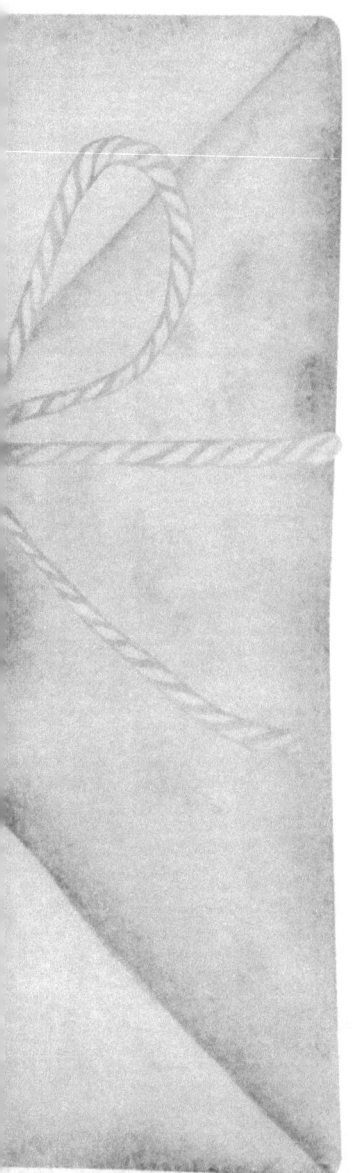

If all the gifts in all the world
were lined up all for me,
'twould not compare with all the love
that I have for thee.

I'd rather have your affection
than things money can afford.
I'd prefer to live each day,
just knowing I'm adored.

Quarantine

I'm breaking protocol,
I can't stand it anymore...
you have no idea...
I want to go to your door.

To wrap my arms around you
and pinch your gorgeous cheeks,
it is your smile, your banter,
your companionship I seek.

I'm so forlorn at this situation,
the madness that we're in,
makes it seem that seeing you
has been made to seem a sin.

My soul be damned!
I'm wasting away –
while completely missing you,
I want to be happy finally,
I'm so tired of feeling blue.

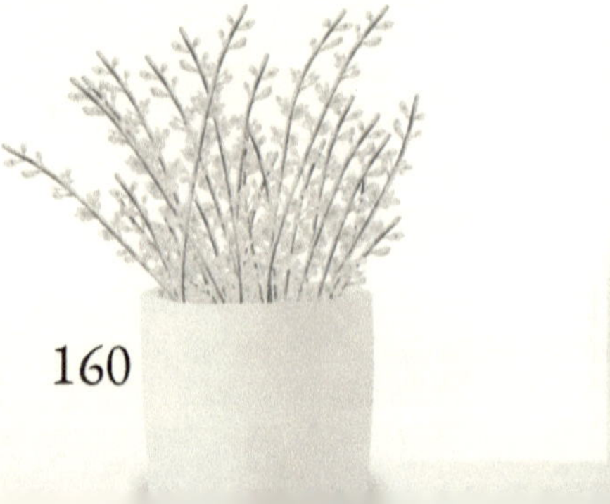

WHERE BEAUTIFUL LOVES *II*

My Favorite

You simply allowing me to love you—
has taught me it's okay to love myself.
You have given me a reason to rejoice,
to look for the silver linings.

You are the most wonderful human I know.
Every day I wake up thankful to know you,
grateful to have found my voice.

Who knew that you'd end up giving me
a completely different type of voice lesson
than either of us could have ever expected?!

I'm not sure how I ever got so incredibly lucky,
"but somewhere in my youth or childhood,
I must've done something good."

Of all that I am grateful for,
you are at the top of my list.
I love you so incredibly much,
and I like you even more than that!

You are my favorite!
I'm here to stay as long
as you'll have me in your company.

BRANDY LANE

Only One

There is only one person on the planet
who makes me smile in that certain way:
gets my brow to unfurrow
and makes my face to relax and unwrinkle.

He puts me at ease
like no drug or alcohol could,
and makes me laugh
as though he invented laughter.

Nothing else matters
when I'm in his company,
it's just us
throughout all time.

If...

If I'd never met him...
I wouldn't have learned to play
so many fun games.
I wouldn't have choreographed
or sang a made-up solo.
I wouldn't be obsessed with dresses
(I hadn't bought one in 16 years).
I wouldn't have sung with the Getty's.
I wouldn't have seen "Something's Rotten."
I wouldn't have written poetry.
I wouldn't have published a book.
I wouldn't have pieces in a bunch of anthologies.
I wouldn't have friends all over the world.
I wouldn't be doing live shows
several times a week.
I wouldn't have
so many wonderful memories.
I wouldn't have remembered
what it felt like to love,
and be loved in return...
even if it was
only for a moment.

Enough

I'm a silly girl. It's funny how, on occasion,
memories just pop up from the crevices of my mind.

The way I used to procrastinate,
just to walk you to your car...
shuffling quickly, pretending not to be gasping for
breath to keep up with your brisk pace.

Within those moments were some of the most intelligent
conversations I would have in a week!
Realizations happened in the flurry, encouragement,
self-awareness.

I ask myself questions constantly now...
holding myself accountable for my thoughts,
you see for my entire life; I was questioned.
And, being a people-pleaser, I caved
to what everyone else thought I should do.

I love the way you don't stand for that.
I love the way that you've made me realize that
I have a voice!

WHERE BEAUTIFUL LOVES II

Never in a million years,
did I have it in my mind
that anything I said or did
was truly important.
I never thought my words
would resonate with anyone.
You were the exception.

You gave me hope when I had none,
you taught me that I am allowed to express
my feelings, and opinions,
as well as
fantasies and desires.
You gave me a place to grow and be safe.

Here are the cleansing tears,
the ones that make me grow,
the ones that are not painful, but beautiful.

Here I sit with the realization
that I am worthy.
I can speak,
and my words are not
unimportant.

BRANDY LANE

Lemon Polish

Lemon furniture polish.
That's right – that's the scent that reminds me of you.
Of all of the crazy things!

There's no soap, no cologne, no tobacco, or coffee...
nothing else has ever stood out except...
lemon furniture polish!

It's gotten to the point where I spend
quite some time polishing my table,
because it reminds me of you.

The spritz of waxy, lemony zest,
smearing across the grain of wood.

I breathe in the citrus afterthoughts dreamily
as I make small circles gleam to a shine.
I sometimes see my reflection and catch myself in a smile,
thinking of you.

I've held you in my arms,
kissed you subtly on the cheek,
sat beside you for hours watching a symphony,
and never once can I say
that I remember your scent.

That part of my mind goes completely blank!

I was trying hard to recall
what you smelled like,
but it eluded me!

It was quite by accident the day that I realized
that waxing my table reminded me of you.

You see, every time we were over,
you'd dust off the table and the place mats
with that lemony freshness.

*I get excited when I smell it now,
it makes me hopeful
that you are coming over,
it is the one scent that completely
reminds me of you.*

BRANDY LANE

Just One More

"Just one more" of everything
is all I'll ever need.
Just one more game,
just one more hug,
just one more poem to read.
It's not that I am greedy
it's just I love you so.
So "one more day of everything,"
I'd like, before I go.
Just one more conversation
so I can look upon your face.
Just one more chance to hold you
in a warm embrace.
Just one more meal to feast on,
one more cake to bake.
Just one more glance across a room
for you my breath to take.
One more time to hear my name
with your rolly rrrr's.
One more time to look up at the sky
to gaze upon the stars.
One more song to sing,
one more symphony.
One more time to sit and relax
and just be you and me.

Stay

My thoughts will celebrate the day
the moment that you came my way...
The only words I wish to say...
to you are these, "please, stay."

I want to love you even more
so to you I must implore,
don't go away and close the door
there's so much more here to explore.

The blooms you've nourished are ready now
so to you, I must avow...
If you can find a way somehow,
release this worry from my brow.

Just say you'll stay and never leave!
Give my heart and mind reprieve...
I promise you, that I'll believe...
and to my soul, your vow receive.

BRANDY LANE

Fallen World

In this fallen world,
we are as clover,
struggling to grow
in the cracks
of the concrete,
reaching for the sun,
and trying not to be
trampled by hurried feet.

Begging to be seen,
 lest we be nibbled up
 by Lagomorphs
 or tickled by
 Lepidoptera's tiny feet.

I see you over there
and will continue to cheer you on—
although I too am waist-deep
in ash, gravel,
and chewed-up blobs of gum
all over these big-city streets.

Feeling discarded when alone,
 trying to tell myself
that I'm somehow important
 while looking at
 every other human speck
 on the planet,
 feeling small—
at least until I remember
that we are all in this together.

WHERE BEAUTIFUL LOVES *II*

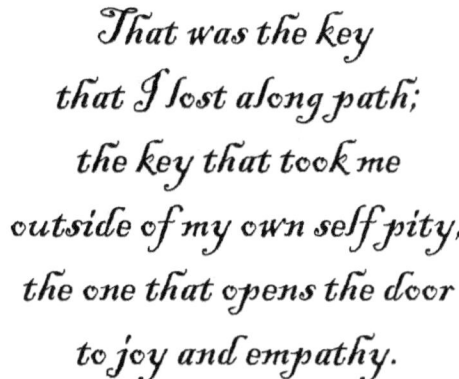

That was the key
that I lost along path;
the key that took me
outside of my own self pity,
the one that opens the door
to joy and empathy.

The one that reminds me
that I am not alone.

Romantic Daydream

If...

I was irresponsible and just went by my feelings alone, I would run away to a cabin in the woods somewhere, and write books with you by my side. We would have that cocoa by the fire and practice all of the interesting shapes we can make with our mouths together.

I'd imagine cozying up on the sofa, with your head in my lap, so I could run my fingers through your hair and stare at your wonderful face. I would trace your features and glide my fingertips down the sides of your neck to massage your strong shoulders.

I would take pleasure in finding succulent recipes to entice your tongue, and read you eloquent stories to intrigue your mind. I would stare into your eyes for hours, and just mingle with your soul. I would ever so gently, playfully, and lovingly caress your hand with my fingertips until you were inundated with desire.

My goodness, that sounds absolutely delightful. The scent of the pines and the earth wafting on the breeze through the open windows. The sounds of breakfast sizzling on the cast iron with all of its savory, tantalizing flavors... feeling your arms wrapped around me as I gently flip the eggs and turn the bacon!

I burn my finger as bacon grease pops from the skillet onto my flesh and let out a whimper... You take my hand and lick off the grease before guiding me to the cold water from the nearby river. You care for me, you look at me as no one ever has... and in that moment, I know I'm loved more than I have ever known.

We lie on the grassy bank and stare up at the puffy white clouds against the cerulean blue. I never want to leave this moment, alas the smell of bacon burning lures us quickly back inside. I serve up the eggs and what's salvaged from the bacon, as you get the coffee and toast...
and in our tiny cottage, in the middle of nowhere...

Sigh.

I have so much more than words.

Hard Candy

He rolls my name
around in his mouth like
it's a piece of hard candy...
tonguing it carefully
so as not to bite —
letting it melt slowly
and flavorfully.
I love it when I hear my name
tumble from his lips...

That Charming Bard

*the writer I have come to know —
and love

Storyteller

When I think of you as of late,
I imagine you up late into the night,
with words as tangible little blocks
floating 'round you in the air.
You pluck them one by one
and place them in a white circle.

They morph into scenery,
into characters and props,
and even the weather bends to your will.
You are the master of the kingdoms
of your mind, a creator of realms.
You are a storyteller.

I just wanted you to see yourself,
as I see you at a moment's glance.
Sure, you are human and normal
and can be pretty unremarkable,
but I see your magic in the middle of the night...
when no one else is looking.

BRANDY LANE

Outside My Window

As if waking from a dream, I lie in bed and stare at olive walls. Gauzy light beams through the atmosphere. I rub my bleary eyes, still not quite sure if I'm awake or still in slumber. The nearly noon sun beckons me to gaze out the open window.

Feeling rather safe, my wallet rests on the sill near the open window. I feel a sense of home and more rested than I've felt in years... although sleep evades me even more now! Who wants to sleep with all this beauty? Even the stars at night call to me.

A picture painted by God himself with added flair by Gesualdo, is framed with mahogany wood. I reach to touch - realizing I am indeed awake as my hand goes through the unscreened rectangle into the cool air.

Could it be? The castle I've dreamt of? Lived out in my mind and fantasies as I've delved into the history that haunts me? Being in anguish and in love, empathetic to the emotions of a nearly five hundred-year-old tale of woe?

Picturesque, the quiet is rather becoming. I realize how much chatter is in my head, usually fighting to get out above all the clutter and responsibilities around me. I savor the peacefulness for a moment. I am overwhelmed and grateful, as a tear escapes.

My stomach growls and coffee is awaiting my arrival. After all, everything in Italy is done with an artistic flair, if something's not excellent, it just isn't worth having. Completely different from the cardboard hurriedness of living in the states.

I sit and ponder everything that has brought me to this point. Enjoying the quiet, the breakfast, the ease of everything around me. The smiles on everyone I encounter... and I say to myself, "I woke up with a castle outside of my window! What could be better than that?"

BRANDY LANE

Tell the Story

The golden hour sunbeams
glinting of the castle walls...
the secrets that are held inside,
echoes of a faltered genius's past.

Horses racing up the cobblestone way
intuition coming to fruition...
climbing the stairs and catching "them"
in ecstasies' height.

Harpsichord echoes through the air
a shrill scream as bones break
as bodies tumble down
the winding marble stairs.

Oh, but to atone!
Trade one sin for another?
I shall punish myself in pleasurable pain
for surely the mouth of Hell is open wide already!

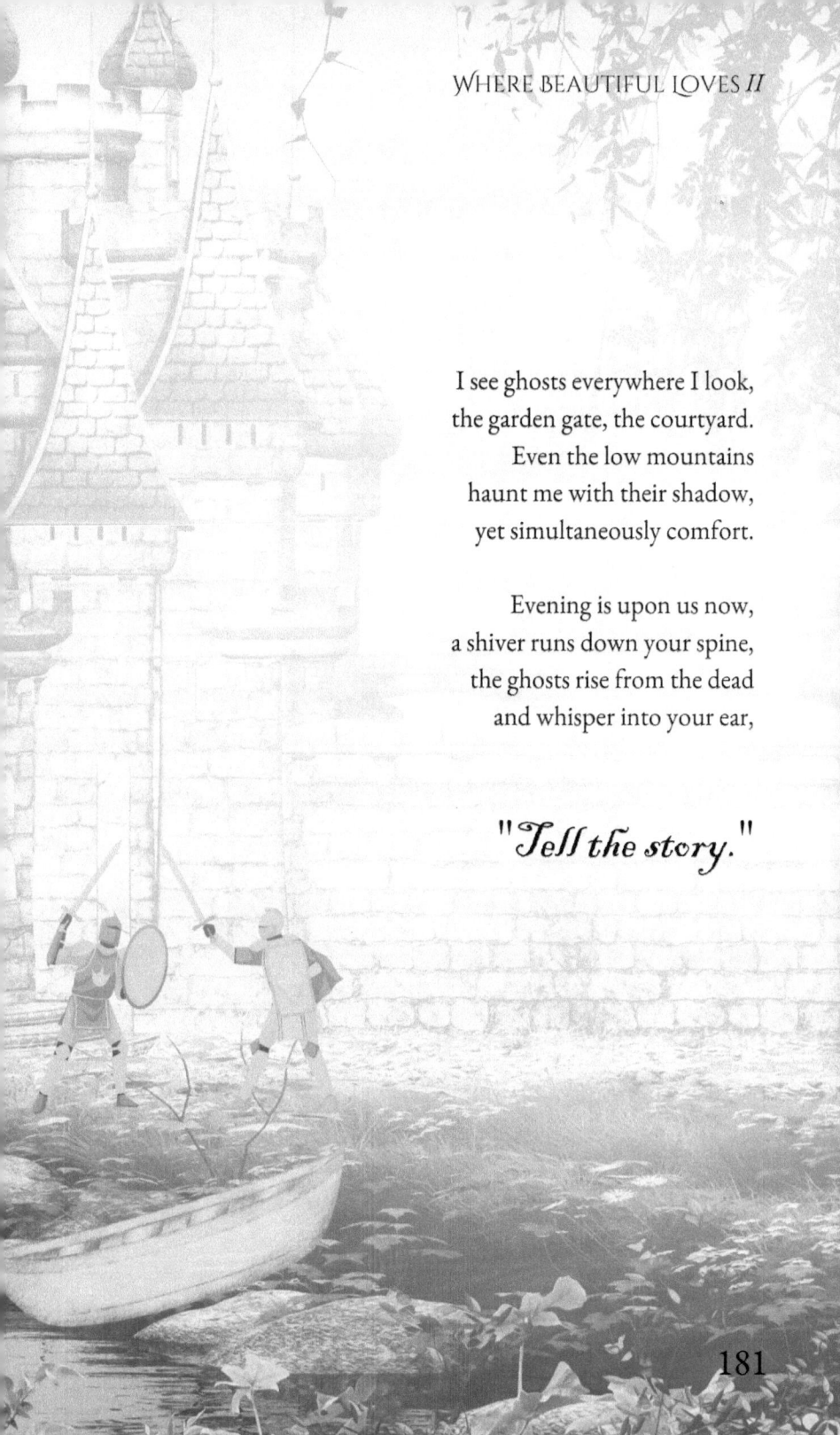

WHERE BEAUTIFUL LOVES *II*

I see ghosts everywhere I look,
the garden gate, the courtyard.
Even the low mountains
haunt me with their shadow,
yet simultaneously comfort.

Evening is upon us now,
a shiver runs down your spine,
the ghosts rise from the dead
and whisper into your ear,

"Tell the story."

BRANDY LANE

On My Mind

There's a man on my mind all of the time.
I imagine him sipping his wine ready to dine
looking out from the patio
where he finds respite from the day.

He's settled under the golden rays
of the Tuscan sun,
amongst the rolling hills
of muted greens and Cypress trees
capped by clear blue skies.

He is surrounded by beauty
but spends most of the day within his mind.
He goes where we are only welcome
after the portal is opened.

When he writes his scripts,
he shares his dreams,
the movie that plays in his mind.
He writes to tell the stories of long ago,
to resurrect the dead.

He tells the stories, I tell you of him.

WHERE BEAUTIFUL LOVES *II*

You see, I've been through those portals,
and like a Disney theme park, based on reality.
I crave to spend more time meandering there.
His mind is a wonderland,
a different magic than most recognize—
but magic all the same.

He makes history relatable.
This is a sacred endeavor,
a hope to bring knowledge to mankind.
To not just tell the story,
but to create an inner monologue,
to not repeat the atrocities that quietly haunt the past.

BRANDY LANE

Roaming

As you delight in the old world
with cappuccinos with foam,
I am traipsing around the new one
finding new places to roam.

No creature-comforts with me
I'm pretty much on my own
A vagabond of sorts,
with nary a place to call home.

I suppose I'll find some things
to make habits in this place, too
maybe find new friends,
but no one can replace you.

To me you are a compass,
my soul points me to yours.
No matter where I seem to be,
it's you my heart adores.

A Sense of Longing

*the distance between us

BRANDY LANE

Crave

Craving, wanting, needing you,
nothing quenches this thirst.
I could try each thing on Earth,
I'll always be wanting you first.

Excursions to the kitchen
when I'm hungry late at night,
no wine, no cheese, no sugary things
can satisfy this plight.

So I've drunk the wine and ate the chips
and here I am again,
Desiring to be with you
but there's always a wrench in my plan.

WHERE BEAUTIFUL LOVES *II*

This time it is an ocean,
and an awful lot of land...
keeping me from seeing you,
and guarding me from your hand.

Whatever can I do with this?
I'm in starvation mode!
There must be some great riddle
that I can decode!

Just send me a portal,
that I can step inside—
all I need to be with you,
is a dream to be my guide!

I lay my head on my pillow,
and finally find the door,
and get to hold you in my arms,
till daylight comes once more.

Tell Me Not To

Tell me not to go.
That's all I want to hear!
I want you to tell me to stay,
because you want me near.

Tell me not to leave!
That's all you have to say...
to tell me that you love me
so I won't go away.

WHERE BEAUTIFUL LOVES *II*

Irreplacable

I'm dying inside!
I don't know how
I'm going to do this
without you near.

I adore you in ways
that I've never experienced,
with anyone else,
and no experience
will ever be the same.

You are irreplaceable.

BRANDY LANE

1000 Miles

Sometimes, I wonder
if you are just a dream.

You seem so real.

The way you make my heart leap,
just by your smile.

I could bury my face in your chest,
and live there, all safe and comforted—
just listening to you breathe.

This longing knows no distance,
for it is the same, whether I am in your arms
or a thousand miles away.

WHERE BEAUTIFUL LOVES *II*

The Train

The lonely whistle of the train
cries longingly of home.
It travels fast and far and wide,
and through the cities roams.

Each time I hear it's brazen sound,
I feel a bit unraveled.
To think of all the many miles
that the train has traveled.

Pondering the sights and sounds,
the traffic that it's stopped,
the many loads of packages
and passengers it's dropped.

I think of how easily
I could hop a train,
and pray that it goes by your house,
so I could see you again.

I'd sit with cows or cars or coal,
uncomfortable for miles.
If it would mean my destination
was in proximity of your smile.

BRANDY LANE

You are Missed

I long for the days of not long ago,
where I could come frolic and play,
and we could banter and laugh a lot
and drink all of the wine away.

I miss your eyes, your knowing glances,
the way you make me feel.
How the butterflies move, and my heart dances,
and nothing around me seems real.

I miss your embrace, your handsome face,
and your curly lashes, too.
Your gorgeous smile (there's no denial),
I miss your untied shoes!

I miss the music we used to make—
you, seeing my inner soul.
I miss the camaraderie we share,
how you always make me feel whole.

How I miss the doting attention,
the compliments, the game.
But the one thing I miss more than anything?
Oh, the way you say my name!

WHERE BEAUTIFUL LOVES *II*

I miss the teasing, the cookies, the fun.
I miss speaking of things such as the Blue Nun.
I miss your cat, purring at my feet.
I miss you hugging me when we first meet.

I savor each moment we've ever had.
You're at the top of my list—
of the most favorite beings in my life,
which is probably why you are missed.

Chivalrous

Thank you is not adequate,
nor would be a rose,
so once again I'm writing you
in very simple prose.

The storms are all around me now,
my life seems a disgrace,
and all I have to comfort me
are mem'ries of your embrace.

The rolling thunder is booming now,
it's hard even to hear.
My face is wet as anger—
drips down with every tear.

Where do I even go from here?
What direction do I run?
It seems there is no easy choice,
no vict'ry to be won.

WHERE BEAUTIFUL LOVES II

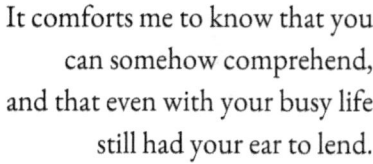

It comforts me to know that you
can somehow comprehend,
and that even with your busy life
still had your ear to lend.

I look to you as a safe place
to rest my weary mind.
The energy it takes to write to you
is refilled every time.

I know you will not hurt me,
as many men might do.
Somehow, I know that in your soul,
you're chivalrous through and through.

I simply ask, as long as we're friends,
say my name as you always do.
Because the day you say it with curses is
the day I'll know we're through.

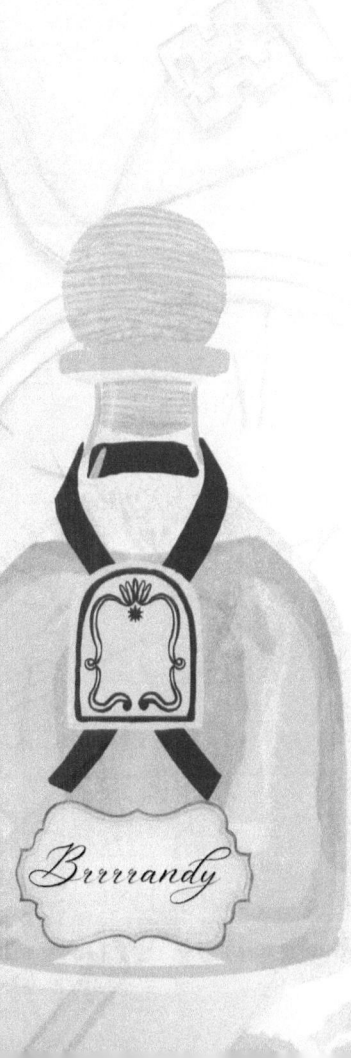

Your Favorite Things

I want to know
your favorite things—
do you like long walks
and dragonfly's wings?

When it's just after dusk,
the sky's shade of blue?
Or perhaps periwinkle
or a different hue?

Do you like tangerines,
or guava, or prunes?
Do you prefer techno
or classic show tunes?

The sound of crickets
on a summer's eve?
Or do you wish
they'd just up and leave?

WHERE BEAUTIFUL LOVES *II*

Sand on the beach
between your toes?
The sound of the trees
as the cool wind blows?

The rumbling sound
of thundering rains?
The lonely whistle of
traveling trains?

I want to know
what makes you tick!
What makes you laugh,
what makes you sick?

I want to know you
so much more—
because you are
the one I adore.

BRANDY LANE

Like No One Else

Sometimes I forget who I am...
then you come along beside me,
and it's like you're right here,
even though we're miles apart.

Your words lift my head,
we see eye to eye, soul to soul.
You don't need to tell me anything
other than to just be myself.

You comfort me like no one else.

An Inspiration

The morning sun against the beautiful blue sky,
reminds me of the way light dances in your eyes.
You have become so dear to my heart,
a part of my soul—it's as if all of these years,
I didn't know what it was that was missing from me,
and now it's as if you have been there all along.

Your name still fascinates me,
in its nearly regal beauty.
You wear it like a crown and,
even when playful (and a little naughty)
you still have an air of respect about you, somehow.

I feel safe and comforted by you,
and know that you would let no harm come to me.
I am bathed in an otherworldly sense of beauty around you.
Your many compliments fill me to the brim,
and for the first time in my life,
I feel worthy of them.
You actually mean what you say,
they are not merely words,
but affirmations of your perceptions.

I'm in constant awe of your ability
to always find the light, to keep moving,
to prove the world and all of its negativity wrong.
You are a beacon for my weary soul,
and an inspiration to my mind.

BRANDY LANE

Better Days Are Coming

Meandering thoughts give me
moments of relief with glimpses of hope.

Memories dance around more quickly,
morphing my frown into a grin.

Melancholy gives way to a giggle, as
mischievously, my simper widens.

Miles will turn to inches
minutes... to seconds when I can see you!

Misty eyes no more shall be,
when you melt into my arms.

Think of Me

Do you ever think of me...
in the quiet when I'm not there?
Do you ever miss my laugh,
My perfume in the air?
Do you wonder what I'm up to
when you don't hear from me...
or if today I'm having coffee,
or drinking some hot tea?

Do you ever reminisce
over moments that we've shared
letters written back and forth,
showing that we cared?
Because sitting here in the quiet.
that's all I can do,
is wonder if you think of me
as oft as I think of you.

BRANDY LANE

When I'm Gone

Will you remember me when I'm gone...
the way I smiled as laughter filled the air?
Will you recall me whilst playing a song...
or when you see someone fixing their hair?

Will you reminisce of days gone by
when we played games until early morn?
Will you break down and cry sometimes
and be incomprehensibly forlorn?

Will you keep in mind that I love you
no matter the hours or miles?
Will you know that I will always crave
one of your fabulous smiles?

Will you take to heart the effort
it takes me to not write,
every hour of the day...
or each minute of the night?

Will you realize that I broke my heart
on my very own,
that I'll remember you every day
when I'm all alone?

That for a little while I had
the greatest friend I'd known-
and I'm in mourning at how quickly
that the time has flown?

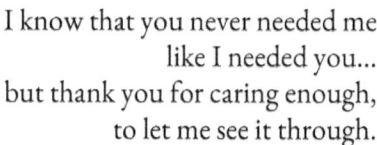

WHERE BEAUTIFUL LOVES II

I know that you never needed me
like I needed you...
but thank you for caring enough,
to let me see it through.

All the little things you do:
each hug, just being there,
each moment simply reminds me
how much you really care.

The closeness that I have with you,
I'll keep wrapped around my heart,
even though, through many miles...
we'll be so far apart.

I'll think about you every day,
as I already do...
and continue always to write books
of poetry to you.

You're not just my muse...
Oh no, you're so much more!
Somewhere in there, I realized
you're someone I adore.

To lose you, I would fall apart:
I would be a mess.
My heart would break, there'd be an ache,
deep within my chest.

So, I will never say goodbye...
because I love you so,
I'll just say "talk to you soon,"
when it's time to go.

BRANDY LANE

24/7 - 365

Don't you know that you will never be
"out of sight, out of mind"?

Do you know why?

Because you are on my mind 24/7-365.

You are always with me...
always.

You aren't someone that I acknowledge
just when I'm just bored or lonely;
you are someone for whom
I move around my schedule.

And if I'm busy?

I get frustrated waiting
for whatever it is I'm doing
to be over with,
just so I can write to you.

When I'm with anybody else?

I'm wishing they were you.

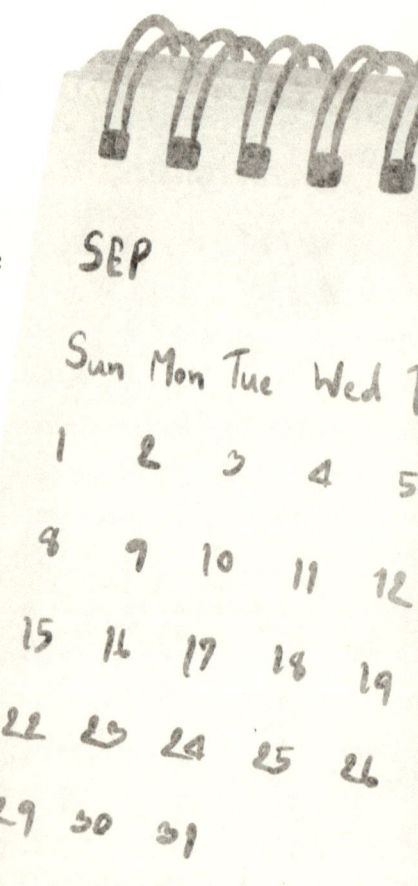

The Dragon Sestinas

*my dragon continually inspires

BRANDY LANE

Dragon (Sestina I)

Now hear a tale about my beautiful friend
whom I refer to as simply, "Dragon".
He has been strong throughout his adventurous life
and lives as a creature of tremendous valor.
For his defense, he wears tough armor,
which only one thing can penetrate—love.

Oh! Not just any love!
The magic lies in the love between friends!
'Tis the only thing that can perforate the thick armor
of this mighty and most glorious Dragon.
In those deemed worthy, filled with valor,
he is bound to them in this earthly life.

Such an adventure is lived throughout life,
when it is full of agape love!
Deeds fulfilled through acts of valor,
bringing closer the bonds of friends...
but the best of them is the Dragon,
once that love has pierced his armor.

The heavy scales of armor,
meant to protect his fragile life...
cover head to toe this Dragon
 and are now greatly perforated with love.
I'll stand with him as his loyal friend
as he strengthens my valor.

WHERE BEAUTIFUL LOVES *II*

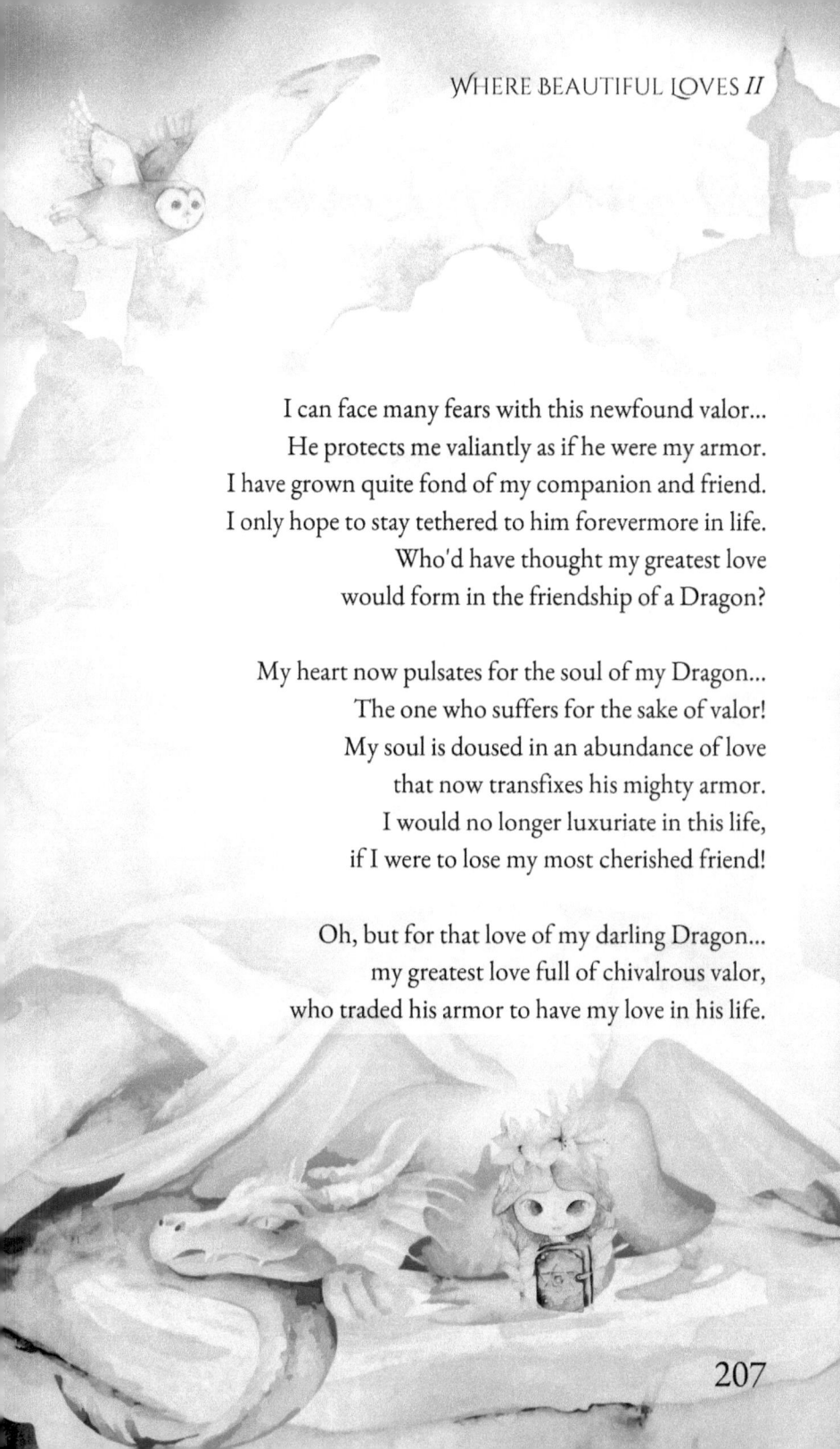

I can face many fears with this newfound valor...
He protects me valiantly as if he were my armor.
I have grown quite fond of my companion and friend.
I only hope to stay tethered to him forevermore in life.
Who'd have thought my greatest love
would form in the friendship of a Dragon?

My heart now pulsates for the soul of my Dragon...
The one who suffers for the sake of valor!
My soul is doused in an abundance of love
that now transfixes his mighty armor.
I would no longer luxuriate in this life,
if I were to lose my most cherished friend!

Oh, but for that love of my darling Dragon...
my greatest love full of chivalrous valor,
who traded his armor to have my love in his life.

Depths of Love
(Sestina II)

A passion from the depths of love,
forged by the fiery dragon.
Burnishing strength to the armor
like the warm hug of an old friend.
Memories of hazy, charred remnants of life
are cherished like badges of valor.

Oh, but to whom do I owe this valor?
'Tis for my dearest love!
For he is the one who saved my life,
and swooped in like a dragon!
I could not have a better friend;
He protects me like resilient armor.

Cumbersome though it seemed, that amour.
Repelling harsh words, restoring my valor.
Its protection became like a friend...
teaching me the discipline of self-love;
I too, became a dragon!
I anticipated a new life.

Before that day, t'was not much of a life...
I had no protection, no armor.
That is when I was saved by my dragon
who protected me with valor.
He taught me not to fear and showed me how to love.
An unconditional and trusting soul, he became my dearest friend.

WHERE BEAUTIFUL LOVES *II*

Just as the Earth has the moon so I now have a friend.
The best angel that God could spare to place into my life:
an unconditional, undeniable, everlasting love
that protects me from the swords, like armor.
I now can hold my head up with valor,
and fly the vast skies with my dragon.

He's always flying above—that dragon,
who's now my dearest friend.
With never-ending valor,
and full of verve for life.
I am now clothed in armor
that is fortified with love.

The foundations of valor are borne through this dragon;
cloaked as the love of my dearest friend.
He valiantly protects my life with his love as armor.

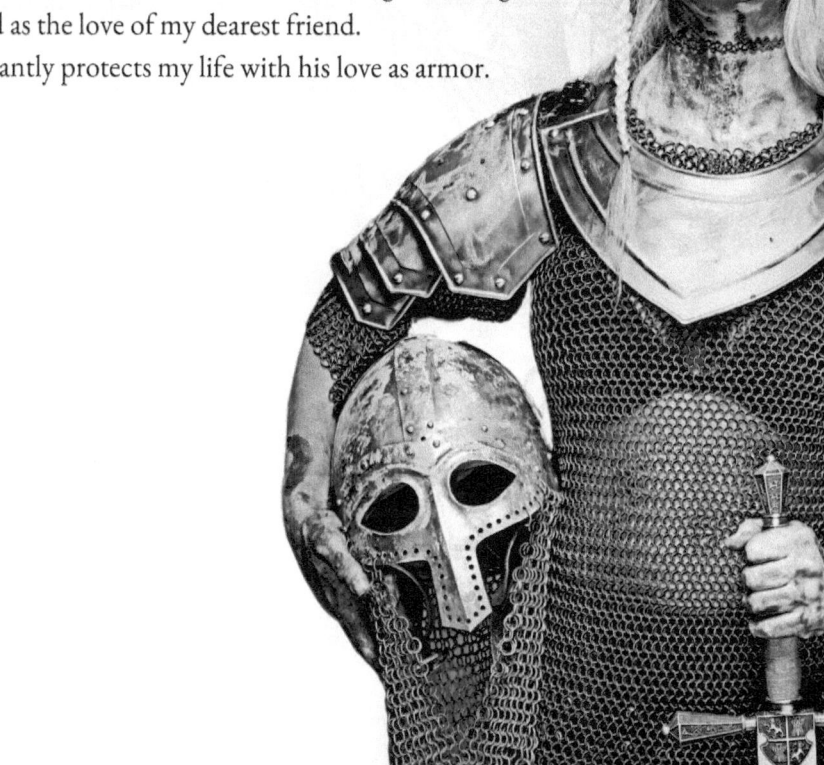

BRANDY LANE

Blue   (Sestina III)

Oh Dragon, I have missed you so!
Tell me stories from long ago!
My love for you has never flown -
if anything, it has vastly grown.
Your piercing eyes which see right through—
my soul, are of the deepest blue.

Whenever I feel blue
I remember how you love me so -
and the doldrums you carried me through
that haunts me from not long ago.
My strength has rapidly grown,
yet my fears have not flown.

Many times, you could have flown
up to skies of brightest blue...
but our bond has only grown
and you've stayed with me, so
as to loyally usher me through—
as you did so long ago.

I'm grateful to have gotten through
my wings have not yet flown—
as in the ages long ago,
up through the skies of brightest blue.
Through the centuries I've loved you so!
The sprinkled seeds of love have grown!

WHERE BEAUTIFUL LOVES *II*

The gardens of my mind have grown
your love has seen me safely through.
In ancient stories shared just so
the memories neither ceased nor flown.
The sky was a familiar shade of blue
that I can't quite place from long ago.

Yet, it does not seem so long ago,
because our love has constantly grown.
I no longer see sadness as being blue.
The blue of your eyes has buoyed me through.
Because of you, doldrums have flown,
and all because you've loved me so.

I remember the blue from not long ago—
maybe from a year or so, but I've since grown.
Joy now carries me ever through,
and my melancholy has flown.

BRANDY LANE

Hell Hath No Fury
(Sestina IV)

It was as if I was being buried alive
each time he spoke his words;
they landed on me and stung my eyes
and choked me of my breath.
When I tried to speak, mud spewed,
and nothing but a gurgle emerged.

Oh, but when it emerged
I felt more alive—
as the muddied disdain spewed.
I refused to let him stifle my words,
I pushed them out with my breath
as mud poured through my eyes.

I seethed hate through my polluted eyes;
Satan himself emerged.
He used my breath
to keep me alive,
and took over my words
as condemnation spewed.

As a volcano, it spewed—
glowing red as the dragon's eyes,
burnishing in fire, my brazen words
emblazoned my soul as it emerged—
somewhere between dead and alive,
as ash flew from my mouth with my breath.

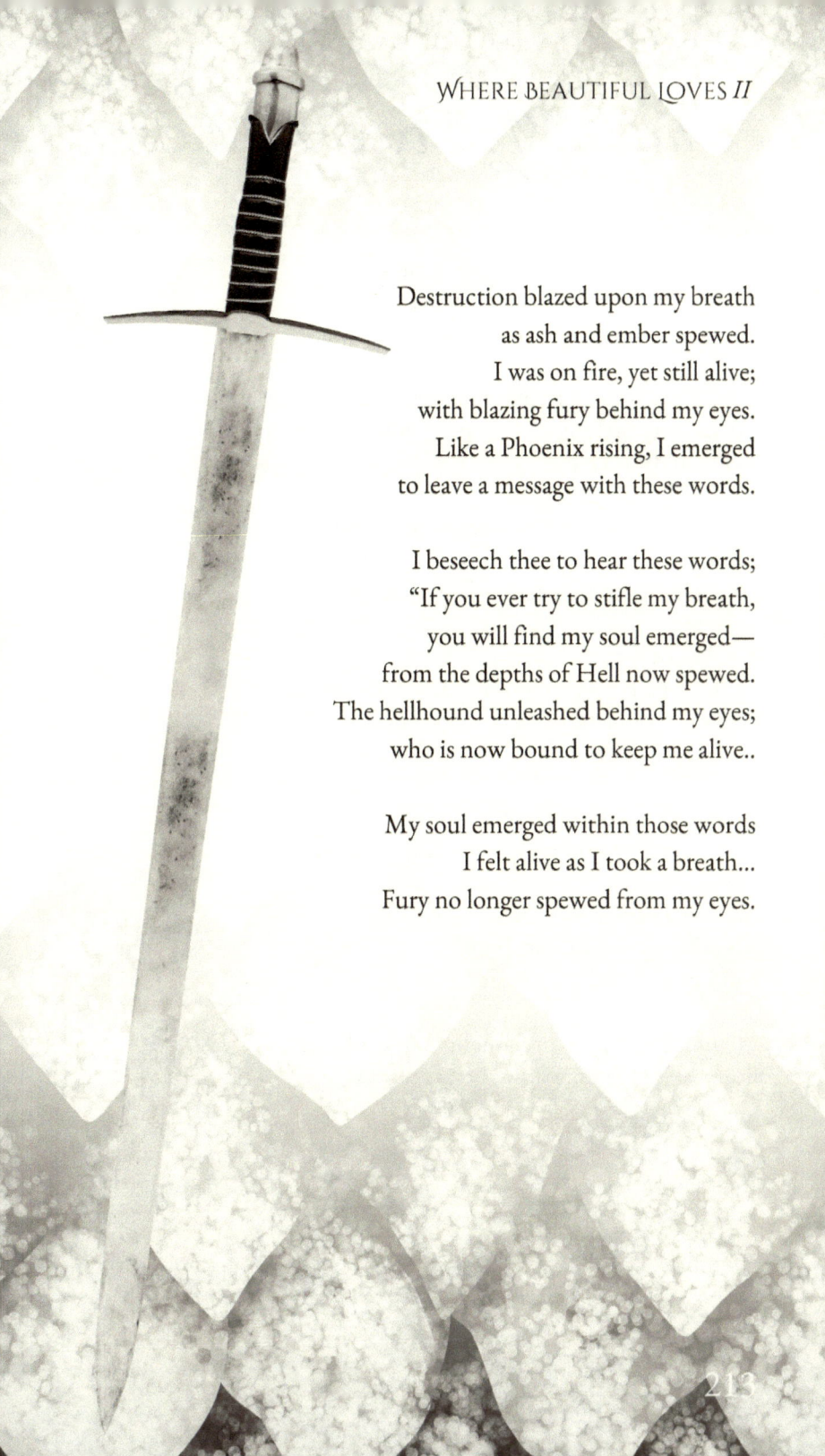

WHERE BEAUTIFUL LOVES *II*

Destruction blazed upon my breath
as ash and ember spewed.
I was on fire, yet still alive;
with blazing fury behind my eyes.
Like a Phoenix rising, I emerged
to leave a message with these words.

I beseech thee to hear these words;
"If you ever try to stifle my breath,
you will find my soul emerged—
from the depths of Hell now spewed.
The hellhound unleashed behind my eyes;
who is now bound to keep me alive..

My soul emerged within those words
I felt alive as I took a breath…
Fury no longer spewed from my eyes.

Thank You to my Muse...

Thank you for allowing me to be myself.
 In all of my weirdness, my wayward emotions,
  my quips of intelligence and naivety as well.

Thank you for not giving up, when I was slipping away...
like an otter drifting and sleeping, you held me close
so I wouldn't get lost.

Thank you for allowing me to escape with you, in my mind.
Even when you were going through the shadows yourself.
Somehow, you still held the lantern for me.

Could I be past the fantasy?
Could it be I'm waking from a fabulous dream?
Will I still think of you as a winged creature,
be it angel, or beast?

Maybe on occasion, I will see the glimpses...
the places my mind took me to keep you safe,
to keep me safe.
My hideaway cave where I used to go
has taken over my entire mind...
and I barely need the cave itself.

My mind flourishes in thoughts and wild ideas
nearly all of the time now.

The mountain climb now has a worn, cleared path...
And flowers and ivy have grown in craggy places.

There's a garden and a village near the foot.
It's no longer a struggle to ever find you.
I don't need to know what you're doing all of the time.
I can meander in the gardens alone,
and know that I will see you sooner or later.

Maybe I'm growing up a little...
and I'm starting to see you as more human
and still my favorite being in the world,
and even though I'm older (ahem) I still look up to you...
Even though you are sometimes flying
by the seat of your pants just as I am.

 Don't think I haven't seen your struggle,
your journey, your tenacity, and your determination...
wanting to throw in the towel,
just to let all of the frustration come out in the wash
just to pick it back up, fresh and renewed.

I may not write as flowery,
and my eyes may not flutter
as they did before,
because this beauty is different.

You're real.
Real things need care and respect,
and are much more precious than fantasy.

Real things can hurt and get hurt...
They can bleed and get damaged,
and they cannot fly.

I will do my best, to care for you in your realness,
just as I did in my fantastical mind when you were on a pedestal.

Will I still sigh on occasion and smile slyly?

Possibly...

Will I still get nervous and act like a complete dolt?

Inevitably.

Will I still look at you on occasion as though
you hold the stars and moon in your eyes?

Sigh... Always

You, somehow, give me a reason to dream,
whilst gluing my feet on the ground.

Well. I'm afraid I must be off.
I've got a million impossible things to do.

                        Always,
                        Brandy

A Letter from the Muse

I told you she'd take me off the pedestal.
T'was inevitable.

The process might not even be complete yet –
but we might try to make it as painless as possible.
The ground is hard at the base of pedestals, you know.

Many of us spend much of life avoiding pain.
But love is pain. Love hurts.
Love empathizes and bleeds.
Love gets scarred and scared.

But let us not spend life avoiding love,
lest we avoid really living.

A butterfly emerges from its chrysalis,
and waits for its wings to dry.
So does a newborn dragon, I imagine,
Poking a curious head through a crack in its hard shell.

It basks a bit in the warmth of the sun,
Takes a deep breath,
and then, with trepidation...

begins to fly.
   Brandy's Dragon

About the Author
Brandy Lane

Brandy Lane has lived most of her life in Indiana and Colorado, where she resides with her husband and four children. She published her first book, *Where Beautiful Loves*, in December 2020 under her imprint, **Where Beautiful Inks**. Just after the release of her first book, she discovered anthologies as an option for publishing and has since had poetry pieces included in over three dozen publications. In 2023, she curated and edited, *Winter, A Poetic Anthology* which is a collaboration of 25 poets from all over the world. It spent 5 days at #1 in New Releases in Anthologies on Amazon.

A hopeless romantic, Brandy draws inspiration mainly from nature, but also from human connection. Her poetry is much like her personality, showing vulnerability as well as strength. The muse that she writes to is someone who taught her she is worthy of love, that she is "enough" and yes, "sometimes more than enough." She finds beauty in every situation, which sometimes is her greatest curse.

In her spare time, she loves spending time outdoors in the mountains, taking in the sublime views. She also loves a good board game, and video chatting with her favorite friends all over the world.

Brandy can be found online: on Instagram @wherebeautifullives and Facebook @Where Beautiful Lives

About the Editor
Reena Doss

"I'll find you in the dark because I'm the girl who loves to stay lost amongst the midnight stars caught up with moonbeams in a lantern trying to find my way back home."

Reena Doss considers writing to be her first voice of expression, followed closely by art and creativity. Through the encouraging platform provided by the Instagram community, she reclaimed her lost voices, evolved a few others and discovered new ones along the way. This has redeemed her trust that consistent Hope, Faith and Love in what is true ignites what is impossible to occur. Her adoration for her beloved Weaver, the Celestial Sky, Nature and her fellow Earthians has given her immeasurable courage to endure every season with a resilience born from battles overcome. She also showcases her artistic talents at His Wild, which features her digital paintings and shares her passion for children's literature at The Pickleton Universe by working on kid lit books for the future. Reena is also the Founder of Ink Gladiators Press where she publishes theme based work in anthologies under the names—Our Earthians Community Group and Translations Of Hope, reviews self-published books and recommends self-publishing services at IGP Ship. Overall, her voices are a reflection of her personality, life story and unwavering faith.

Currently, she resides in Bangalore, India but loves traveling to far-off places inside her head and sometimes, in the world that others call real. You can try and catch her on Instagram at reenadossauthor but it may not always be possible as she is generally off on adventures chasing dragons, phoenixes and mermaids down for stories. www.reenadoss.com

Acknowledgements

So grateful for the editors and publishers who have included the following poems in their anthologies and magazines. The poems, many times in their rawest, and earliest versions, appeared as follows.

"Awash in Candlelight" was originally published in Red Penguin Books *Tis The Season's* (Dec. 2020) p. 61

Also Published In

Poetry 365 by RDW (both abridged and unabridged editions) for November, December, January, February, March, April, May, and June, and special editions of *Creator*, *Hope*, and *Self Portrait* editions.

Red Penguin Books has published her pieces in *'Tis the Season's*, *The Flower Shop on the Corner*, *The Ocean Waves*, and *Bloom Issue 2* magazine.

Clarendon House Publications published her poems in their *Poetica 2* and *Poetica 3* anthologies.

Ink Gladiators Press' anthologies of *The Rise and Fall of Chimera's* and *Gray, We Hide our Colors Within*.

Indie Blu(e) Publishing published a mental health piece in *Through the Looking Glass: Reflecting on Madness and Chaos Within*, and their newest anthology, *But You Don't Look Sick: The Real Life Adventures of Fibro Bitches, Lupus Warriors, and Other Superheroes Battling Invisible Illness*.

300 South Media Group has published her in *As Darkness Falls* and features her first flash fiction piece in *Sunset Rain*. She will also have three pieces included in *Shadow of the Soul*.

Train River Poetry has published her in *Poetry 7*.

Who's Who of Emerging Writers by **Sweetycat Press**.

Harness Magazine in their November 2022 issue.

Silent Spark Press *Amazing Poetry Volume 13, 2023*.

Other books by Brandy Lane

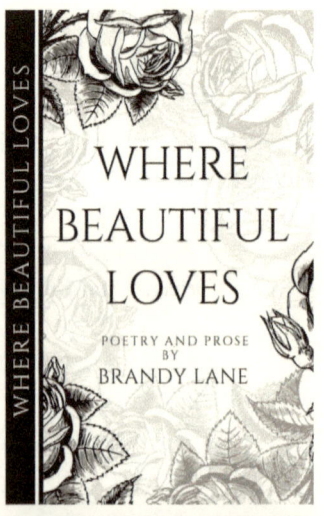

Anthologies by Where Beautiful Inks

Coming Soon!

In the Works

www.ingramcontent.com/pod-product-compliance
Lightning Source LLC
Chambersburg PA
CBHW060557080526
44585CB00013B/603